THE COMPASSIONATE CONNECTION

THE
COMPASSIONATE
CONNECTION

The Healing Power of Empathy and Mindful Listening

DAVID RAKEL, MD

with Susan K. Golant, MA

W. W. Norton & Company
Independent Publishers Since 1923
New York · London

The Compassionate Connection is a work of nonfiction, but names and other potentially identifying characteristics of the individuals depicted have been changed. Meditation techniques and practices described are not intended as a replacement for medical advice or psychotherapy. Please seek the advice of a qualified physician or therapist if you are experiencing symptoms of emotional or physical illness. As of press time, the URLs displayed in text link or refer to existing third-party Internet sites and conditions existing on those sites at the time of publication. The publisher and the author are not responsible for any content on third-party sites.

For information about permission to reproduce selections from this book, write to Permissions, W. W. Norton & Company, Inc., 500 Fifth Avenue, New York, NY 10110

For information about special discounts for bulk purchases, please contact W. W. Norton Special Sales at specialsales@wwnorton.com or 800-233-4830

Manufacturing by Quad Graphics Fairfield
Book design by Dana Sloan
Production manager: Anna Oler

Library of Congress Cataloging-in-Publication Data

Names: Rakel, David, author. | Golant, Susan K., author.
Title: The compassionate connection : the healing power of empathy and mindful listening / David Rakel, MD, with Susan K. Golant, MA.
Description: First edition. | New York : W.W. Norton & Company, [2018] |
Includes bibliographical references and index.
Identifiers: LCCN 2017056375 | ISBN 9780393247749 (hardcover)
Subjects: LCSH: Healing—Psychological aspects. | Compassion. | Interpersonal relations—Health aspects. | Interpersonal communication—Health aspects. | Mind and body.
Classification: LCC R726.5 .R33 2019 | DDC 610.1/9—dc23
LC record available at https://lccn.loc.gov/2017056375

W. W. Norton & Company, Inc., 500 Fifth Avenue, New York, N.Y. 10110
www.wwnorton.com

W. W. Norton & Company Ltd., 15 Carlisle Street, London W1D 3BS

1 2 3 4 5 6 7 8 9 0

For our valued connections . . .

My wife Denise and our children Justin, Lucas, Sarah, and
her husband, Adam

and

My husband Mitch, our children, and grandchildren

CONTENTS

Introduction

As human beings, we are born with an innate and nearly limitless capacity for caring and compassion. We recognize when others around us are hurting; as the latest neuroscience has shown, we quite literally feel their pain—imaging studies have demonstrated that the same networks in the brain are activated whether people receive a painful stimulus themselves or are merely witnessing someone else receiving it.[1] And we want to help. In fact, the human brain is actually wired for cooperation and giving.[2] But we're not always good at it. We say the wrong things, or we zero in on the wrong problems. Often we manage to do more harm than good, causing hurt feelings and even damaging relationships.

But there is another way. In *The Compassionate Connection: The Healing Power of Empathy and Mindful Listening*, I explain that we all have the astounding ability to help others in a way that prompts their healing from within and strengthens our bonds with them—while doing emotional and physical good for ourselves in the process. Indeed, some social psychologists have theorized that giving may enhance the giver's self-interest more than receiving.[3] This is a two-way street.

As the founder and director of the University of Wisconsin's integrative medicine program, and now professor and chair of the department of Family and Community Medicine at the University of New Mexico, I have discovered that people become the most effective caregivers when they use the vital yet surprisingly low-tech tool of human connection. A wide array of research now demonstrates that we humans can use our very presence to promote health in those who are ailing and guide them on a path toward recovery.

My colleagues and I studied this connection in the primary care clinic at the University of Wisconsin Medical Center. We taught doctors to interact with patients using techniques of deep listening and empathy. We found that those who experienced a connection with their doctor recovered from the common cold a day faster than those who didn't. This wasn't just feel-good therapy; there was physiological evidence of the effect. Patients who felt a connection actually produced increased levels of disease-fighting immune cells.

Making the connection involves particular skills everyone can learn and apply. Becoming present "in the moment" with another person (not an easy task in today's fast-paced, noisy world) and deep listening enable people to establish trusting relationships and exchange meaningful information. This kind of rapport allows helpers to bring their best to the service of others and may simply "stack the deck" in favor of healing. Indeed, studies have shown that the connection, once having been established, may also help address unhealthy eating habits, resistance to exercise, chronic health problems, the efficacy of cancer treatments, depression, and even the deleterious effects of premature birth.

In this book, I draw upon my clinical experience and my own research, as well as thirty years of published studies in major medical journals—in the fields of medicine, sociology, psychology, meditation, and neuroscience—to describe the effect of the human connection and the ways it can be used to boost health. I use examples from my years of practice to demonstrate the basis of each technique that makes the connection possible.

. . .

As a practitioner of family, rural, and integrative medicine, I have encountered myriad hyphenated terms that seek to describe the mechanisms by which this discipline can have its greatest effect. A couple that come to mind are bio-psycho-social medicine and psychoneuroimmunology (a relatively new multidisciplinary area that investigates how stress affects the nervous and immune systems). Each of these aims to express a simple concept that we may already understand intuitively: the mind and body are intertwined physiologically in ways that affect health—for better and for worse. Indeed, I have come to see that we can't treat one without treating the other. Moreover, it has been scientifically proved that a person's capacity to feel beauty and awe, and his or her ability to turn inward to find meaning and purpose, also improve health and well-being. This is a part of the "mystery" and the "art" of healing, that when aroused in others and coupled with science leads to more positive outcomes. Not only does this happen within and throughout one human being but also among human beings. Positive contagion can spread throughout communities. But before individuals can promote a more global connectedness to healing, they need to develop it within themselves.

In Part I of *The Compassionate Connection*, I cover the power people possess to connect to others and make a difference in their lives. I delve into the importance of a compassionate connection for recovery and examine how it can enhance the placebo effect, or what I prefer to call the "healing effect"— a person's capacity for self-healing. We will look closely at the latest neurobiological research on the physiological underpinnings of the connection to gain an understanding of how and why it works. And we'll examine why it's necessary to recruit a patient's health from within, and how people bungle opportunities to help and consequently rupture the connection they're so ardently trying to make.

In Part II, I elucidate the tools that are necessary to create the connection. In order to truly be of service, helpers must know themselves and acknowledge their own biases before approaching another human being. Moreover, the mind's constant internal chatter or "clutter" can interfere with clearly seeing what another person actually needs, so we will look at how to set aside this clutter and be "present." Because nonverbal communication can draw people closer, I will examine how we create connections with our bodies and facial expressions. Deep listening can help caregivers unearth another's authentic story—one that may not be evident on the surface of interactions. Caregiving can be exhausting, so I will focus on the sources of burnout and ways to avoid it that include the positive aspects of meditation. And finally, I will show you how to notice unexpected beauty in authenticity—even if it means fully facing suffering. In this process of connection, we gain clarity, creativity, wisdom, and even good health for ourselves.

SERVING . . . WITH COMPASSION

With the explosion of information technology, gadgets and equipment, and electronic record keeping, tech is becoming increasingly prominent in our health delivery system. Soon, when we stand on the bathroom scale, all of our bio-measures will show up on the mirror or our smartphones. We will also be able to check our unique DNA profile to determine whether we metabolize one medicine better than another. But technology and Big Data algorithms, wonderful as they are, will never have insight or intuition. They will never understand how to facilitate healing within complex biological and emotional systems. This is a uniquely human talent.

This book honors that human connection. Through it, caregivers can inspire others to have hope, resolve, and determination to make—and stick with—a health-oriented plan. The best part, however, is that the connection becomes a win-win situation for everyone. Even as it boosts health and enhances wellness, it strengthens relationships by removing judgment and deepening trust. It lessens caregivers' stress, reduces burnout, and improves resiliency. In fact, those who connect with others—whether as spouses, parents, friends, medical providers, coworkers, business leaders, or politicians—not only communicate better and become more helpful individuals but also invariably experience a sense of gratification and even joy.

Dr. Rachel Naomi Remen, author of *Kitchen Table Wisdom*,

makes a great comparison between helping and serving. She suggests that when people "help," they ask for something in return, as in "I have helped you, now what are you going to do for me?" But when they "serve," they also serve themselves because in addressing the needs of another, they address their own. Indeed, in service, we all become part of a larger whole. In this way, *The Compassionate Connection* has the power to improve the quality of our lives and the lives of those around us.

PART I

Our Healing Power

1

Compassion Hastens Healing

What kind of doctor do I need to be for this patient today?
—MICHAEL BALINT, *The Doctor, His Patient and the Illness*[1]

It was a routine Tuesday, and the clinic at the University of Wisconsin in Madison happened to be busy. I was part of a team of nine physicians and twenty-eight other health practitioners, and all combined, we saw about 325 patients a day. We faced time constraints for each visit, and we did our best to keep people from waiting too long. On this particular day, only two hours into the schedule, I was swamped. With a steady stream of patients ahead and multiple tasks still to address for those I'd just seen, the day already had the feel of an avalanche about to give way.

Move efficiently, don't linger, had become the morning's mantra. In the first exam room, a woman in her midfifties was waiting to see me about a pain in her shoulder that had been nagging her for two months. Walking down the hall, I began listing for myself the questions I would ask her and mulling the range of tests she might need. Next door, a young man, a new patient to the clinic, was eager to have me look at an itchy, scaly rash that had surfaced on his arms and down his legs. I hoped, for the sake of time, it would be run-of-the-mill eczema that I could treat with a steroid cream. I paused at a computer to enter an electronic prescription for the patient I'd just seen, a shy teenager with a long history of asthma, when the clinic nurse informed me that the person waiting for me in exam room 3 was Martha. I felt my chest tighten.

It wasn't personal. From the first time I'd treated Martha more than five years earlier, I'd always liked her. She was a good-natured, rosy woman in her early sixties who had come from the same part of the country where I'd grown up, and we often chatted about the changes we'd faced and the regional dishes we'd each missed after moving to the Midwest. She and her family lived in one of the more affluent neighborhoods in town. I had met her husband, who had accompanied her to several appointments, and her son, who was now in graduate school. Martha and I had an easygoing rapport, which was fortunate because she tended to visit the clinic often. She just happened to be one of the more challenging medical cases in my practice.

Martha's health issues were the type that don't fit easily into the typical fifteen-minute appointment. For several years, she had been suffering with rheumatoid arthritis, a complex autoimmune disease that occurs when the body's own immune cells attack the joints. The flare-ups cause swelling, joint disfigurement, and terrible pain. When we treat patients who have rheumatoid arthritis, we rarely rid the body of the disease, but merely knock it into remission by controlling the inflammation. Martha had been on several anti-inflammatory medications, including the steroid prednisone, which helped reduce the swelling, but also came with significant side effects like weight gain. In fact, she had put on so many pounds, her blood glucose was elevated and she now needed to be on diabetes medication. The prednisone had also led to gastritis, an awful stomach irritation, so she was taking an acid-suppressing medication. On top of all that, the condition had severely affected her ability to cope with daily life and resulted in depression. So I put her on the antidepressant Prozac. At her last appointment, we had even added a sleeping aid to her medication regimen because she was having trouble staying asleep through the night. Prednisone, in particular, can trigger insomnia.

This kaleidoscope of complex health problems is not as uncommon as one might think. Many people have medical conditions whose treatment leads to weight gain that then produces a surge of other diagnoses: heart condition, diabetes, back pain, knee injuries, depression, and sleep apnea. Or they have syndromes—chronic pain, lupus, fibromyalgia, or inflammatory bowel disease—with mysterious causes that aren't fully understood for which we can only address the symptoms. These days, a health issue might not be one isolated illness, but a complex tangle of disorders.

When people have so many diagnoses, treating any one of them is like approaching a tower of stacked grapefruits in the produce aisle: you address one aspect of their condition, but then scramble to stop a cascade of others. Managing each problem as a separate entity results in multiple treatments and the risk of the person having to take a wide array of medications. This dangerous situation, an all-too-common occurrence, is called "polypharmacy."[2]

The major concern of polypharmacy is that the medical community has no idea how *all* of these chemicals interact with one another. Indeed, one drug may even counteract another's reason for use,[3] and the drugs can cancel each other out, as I'll explain more fully in Chapter 2. But perhaps more importantly, taking multiple medications like this greatly increases the risk of medical error, which has now been predicted to be the third leading cause of death in the United States, behind heart disease and cancer.[4] How can caregivers evolve beyond the dangerous "find it, fix it" pharmaceutically dominated medical culture they live in? My primary care colleagues and I believe they can do this by developing insight into patients' unique lives to see how their conditions are often interrelated and not separate entities that require a "pill for every ill."

So with all of these issues buzzing around in my mind, I braced myself as I entered the exam room where Martha was waiting.

"Hey, Doc, I see you're running a little late," Martha said in her jovial manner.

I greeted her and asked what had prompted today's appointment. She began to list her latest concerns. They weren't significantly different from the ones she'd had before, though each seemed to have become more onerous. Then she added a new symptom to the mix. With the pressure of time and the enormous complexity of her interlocking disorders and treatments, my mind reeled into a reactive mode: *What's the new diagnosis?*

And what new medication does Martha now need? How will it interact with her other meds and create another layer of problems? Was she really going to be any better off after this visit?

I meant to maintain my composure, but she must have seen a shadow of frustration dart across my face. It was hard to conceal that I was feeling angry with myself—and even a little annoyed with her. Here was an individual who needed something from me, but whose medical problems, all interconnected and seemingly snowballing, were becoming insurmountable. I didn't feel helpful in the least. In fact, I felt that I was failing. Each time she came back to see me, the new solution worsened her status. Was I supposed to send her off with an additional prescription that might present other side effects? On the one hand, I could treat the most recent symptom and deal with the fallout. On the other, I could encourage her to "just live with it," which would leave her feeling as though she had come to me for no reason at all. My sense of powerlessness was devastating.

One thing was clear to me: The problem was not Martha. Rather, it had to do with the focus I was supposed to give to the individual symptoms instead of the big picture of her health. I was expected to "patch" but not to heal, even though what Martha needed was far more than stop-gap fixes. How could it be, in this day and age, that with all my training and the time I had for the appointment I could provide only piecemeal help? At that moment, I realized I wanted to change the way I engaged with all my patients. If I was going to help Martha and other people like her, I would have to learn to understand their disorders in a new way. In fact, to be effective and offer meaningful help, I had to find a way to get closer to the source of the illnesses.

ON BEING OF SERVICE

In the *Descent of Man,* which was published twelve years after *On the Origin of Species,* Charles Darwin had argued that when it comes to human beings, the survival of the kindest is most important—not necessarily the survival of the fittest. He called sympathy the "foundation-stone" of our social instincts.[5] This question of how to be a helpful person—and even more importantly, how to be *most* helpful—has captivated me since childhood. Like most other kids, I first was taught that being helpful meant being kind. Share toys. Give hugs. Be respectful. All good advice. I wouldn't quibble for a second about the importance of treating other people kindly. As I grew older, however, I began to wonder whether there are more nuances in what we can offer as individuals. Kindness can go a long way—and the world we live in certainly needs plenty of it—but I also hoped the service I could provide wouldn't be just a fleeting gesture.

I aspired to be caring in a way that could make a difference. For years, I was so gripped by the idea, I began to see the imperative everywhere. "Give a man a fish and you feed him for a day; teach a man to fish and you feed him for a lifetime," was a proverb that turned up in middle school on a wisp of paper in a fortune cookie and stayed with me for a good long time.

All of this got me thinking about how one person could be the vector for positive change in another. When I chose to become a family doctor two decades ago, I had soaring ambitions along those lines. I had grown up with great role models. My dad is a doctor. In fact, he's one of the founders of the field of family medicine that began in 1969. For years, I was awed by him and my mother, who worked as a nurse. What caught my attention, even as a child, was seeing their warm interactions with patients outside the office. People would greet them on the street with a bear hug, expressing emphatic gratitude, and often adding the most recent development in the personal story of their health—the story in which my parents had played a role. I witnessed remarkable tenderness in these moments and an awareness that something important had transpired because of my parents' assistance. Their involvement had an enduring effect on me. That was what I wanted in a career—the opportunity to offer that magnitude of service, to be honored with the invitation to enter the intimacy of another person's life.

Sure enough, being a family physician is a job that offers ample opportunity to do good. After residency, I became one of two family doctors in a fourteen-bed hospital in the small town of Driggs, Idaho. I felt awe and euphoria when, in a single day, I delivered a baby, treated a heart attack, placed a cast on a teenager's broken arm, and then supported someone who was suffering from depression. How amazing—and what a privilege—it was to participate in such important moments in people's lives. The job put me in contact with patients of every age, from infancy to great-grandparenthood. As they came to see me over the years for regular checkups as well as illnesses, I got to know them for their individual personalities and for their connections in the community, not just for their health problems. I began to build those long-term relationships I had observed in my parents' careers, and to experience the warmth—really, being of service to others—that is the heart and soul of the job.

But the experience wasn't without a few bumps. Some people who came into my office left with the correct medication, but no greater health overall. We would have a pleasant interaction, and I would offer the best medical advice at my disposal, but little would change in their lives. That bothered me. The longer I practiced medicine, the more I began to pay attention to my interactions with my patients and to wonder about those situations that seemed less than fruitful. Even though a person might have gotten a solution to an immediate problem, I still wondered: *Could I have done more? Had I really made a difference for the man with chronic pain? Had I really gotten through to the woman with abnormally high blood sugar?* The day-to-day experience of helping was one thing, but was I really doing the meaningful, enduring kind of good I had hoped to do?

As I became interested in learning about other ways to influence health and healing, I moved on from Driggs. I had heard of a fellowship originated by Andrew Weil, MD, at the University of Arizona on teaching physicians about complementary therapies such as acupuncture and botanicals. At the time, those foundational, health-influencing therapies, as well as nutrition and stress reduction through meditation and spirituality, were considered "alternative" and not mainstream approaches. But Dr. Weil had developed the new field of integrative medicine to stress the importance of incorporating the best of these modalities into our conventional systems of care.

What is integrative medicine? According to the Academic Consortium for Integrative Medicine and Health, it "reaffirms the importance of the relationship between practitioner and patient, focuses on the whole person, is informed by evidence, and makes use of all appropriate therapeutic and lifestyle approaches, healthcare and disciplines to achieve optimal health and healing."[6] Much of the information I had absorbed during my fellowship constellated around how to *stimulate self-healing mechanisms* within my patients' bodies. This is part of what I like to think of as the "mystery and awe" of medicine.

I completed the two-year fellowship and then moved my family to Madison to start an integrative medicine program at the University of Wisconsin where I also continued a medical practice. Like the hospital in Driggs, the clinical care here also offers the opportunity for long-term relationships with patients, but I could also use some of my newly learned skills. Many of these came from self-reflective insight that was encouraged during my fellowship training. This helped me understand that there was more to this healing work than simply prescribing drugs, herbs, or a referral for body work. *I learned the importance of the therapeutic ceremony and how the actual process of delivering care can dramatically enhance the effectiveness of what is prescribed.*

Research now shows how this is possible—that is, how personal interactions can actually have physiological effects on patients. As I will explain more fully in ensuing chapters, the mere presence of others can heighten a person's response to a treatment. For instance, a team, led by neurophysiologist Luana Colloca at the University of Turin in Italy, compared how people fared after surgery when they received pain medication in two distinct scenarios. For some, a nurse entered the room postsurgery and announced that the patient would be getting a powerful analgesic that would make the pain subside in a few minutes. A clinician then arrived and administered the treatment. For a second group, there was no announcement and no one to inject the drug. The patients received the same dose of medication by way of an IV injection from an automatic infusion machine and weren't even informed when the infusion was begun.

Dr. Colloca found that patients receiving the drug by machine needed a *50 percent higher dose of painkiller* than those who anticipated feeling better and received the drug from the nurse. In addition, one hour after treatment, patients on the drip described their pain as "much higher" than those who were given the drug by human hands.[7] The expectancy created ("We are going to give you a pain medication to help you feel more comfortable") and the actual presence of a person giving the medicine significantly enhanced the effect of the medicine. The lived experience is related to much more than just the intrinsic effect of the analgesic. Recent research has shown that positive expectations regarding pain reduces its severity by 28.4 percent, which is the equivalent of an average-size adult taking 8 mg of morphine.[8]

After comprehending more about the power of the interactive process, I started to ask myself fresh questions about how I could more effectively influence healing in another. *Have I been patient enough? Have I been insightful about my patients' circumstances? Have I been imaginative about possible solutions?* And then, there have been cases like Martha's that have been so complex, I've wondered how a merely interactive process could ever contribute to improving such a challenging medical situation.

ALOOF OR EMPATHIC?

The prevailing wisdom in the medical literature for most of the twentieth century asserted that doctors needed to keep their distance to maintain a position of emotional detachment from their patients. In 1912, Sir William Osler wrote in his famous essay "Aequanimitas" that doctors should neutralize their own emotions. That paradigm has held for decades. It was thought that physicians could "study" a patient's inner life by attaining cognitive clarity, a state of sustained emotional divestment. In fact, the topic of disengagement appeared prominently in the *New England Journal of Medicine* and the *Journal of the American Medical Association* in the 1950s and 1960s where it was affirmed that clinical empathy should be based in "detached reasoning"[9]—that is, in order to be most effective in caring for patients, doctors should not get too close to them or connect emotionally to their problems or suffering. In addition, the idea has long held that this so-called objectivity would act as a personal shield. Doctors who were emotionally distant could protect themselves from burning out.

As a result, medical schools taught students how to take a detailed history but didn't always teach them how to connect with patients. That's why, for generations, there's been great tolerance on the medical side for clinicians who are brusque and distant.

This belief has been changing in recent years. Increasing numbers of medical schools are now teaching compassionate care. In particular, they want doctors to learn how to be more connected healers. Having compassion for others doesn't necessarily mean becoming a mess of raw nerves, nor does it entail losing the objectivity to make sound and well-reasoned recommendations. The essence of the compassionate encounter is being able to listen deeply in order to say, "I understand your needs because I see and feel where you're coming from." With compassion, in fact, caregivers can better understand how others interpret their own "health" and how illness affects them. They can better grasp the sources of meaning and purpose in patients' lives.

CAN COMPASSION HELP PEOPLE HEAL?

I believe the answer to this question is yes . . . and that health may ultimately lie in the quality of the compassionate connection that two people create. When individuals perceive a person as caring about them, they may be more willing to open up and express their inner secrets. They may be more available to listen to advice and make changes in their lives.

When we review approaches used by all types of healers throughout history, whether they were doctors or shamans, one consistent pattern stands out. No matter the technologies or medicines available, the healing visit or therapeutic ritual itself has always been critical in an individual's care. The interaction involves elements of hope, trust, wisdom, caring, gratitude, and often, mutual respect. We humans are capable of making each other feel better, even if we have little to offer except reassurance, or sympathy, or merely hand-holding. The surprising thing is that—even before offering any medications or therapies at all—we're capable of improving each other's health.

Look back through medical writing in any era and you'll find evidence of the vital power that humans have—the power of connection. Even in the first-century AD, Hippocrates, known as the father of modern medicine, noted, "For some patients, though conscious that their condition is perilous, recover their health simply through their contentment with the goodness of the physician." Nearly two thousand years later in the late 1800s, the esteemed physician and teacher Sir William Osler, laying the groundwork for twentieth-century medical care, described the fundamentally healthful role of the doctor's bedside manner. Medicine, he wrote, "is an art based on a science."[10] It's that art, he continued, that doctors should cultivate just as much as their stores of medical knowledge.

In 2011, the game show *Jeopardy* pitted their two all-time greatest money winners against IBM's Dr. Watson, a supercomputer that listened to the question and responded just like a human. The contest wasn't even close. Dr. Watson annihilated the two human geniuses. Wellpoint Health Services has now contracted with IBM to place Dr. Watson in many of its outpatient clinic settings. The computer, once as big as a small car, is now the size of a pizza box and is twelve times faster. In the future, I suspect that physicians will no longer be required to remember the various causes of a symptom or abnormal blood test results because they will have these supercomputers to do it for them. But these machines have limitations. How do you program them with the art of connecting?

The funny thing is that even though wise people over the ages have written about this fundamental aspect of healing, we tend to ignore it. Our society doesn't put much stake in the power of the human connection. At least, we don't concertedly and rigorously incorporate *connectedness* into medical care. Instead, we tend to focus our healing hopes elsewhere. Every day, the newspapers trumpet a new device on the market, or a new drug that appears to work better than any previous concoction. We have great interest in technologies that can visualize the interior of the body, like MRIs that reconstruct organs in three dimensions and functional MRI scans that show how areas of the brain light up in real time. We've become a society thirsty for these developments.

Without a doubt, technology has afforded us excellent diagnostic capabilities and treatments. It has given us great appreciation for the complexity of the disease process. Thanks to molecular biology and genetic studies, we now think of various cancers as distinct diseases, each with its own signature and progression. In recent years, we've become more aware that one-size-fits-all treatments are no longer the standard of care, and that medications may need to be fine-tuned for each individual's genome. We know, for example, that people of different races, ages, and genders metabolize drugs differently, and we're even moving toward a time when we can routinely test a person's genome to guide the most effective prescription and cancer treatment, a process referred to as "personalized medicine."

All of these developments are important, and I'm not downplaying their worth. I'm grateful that my patients can benefit from them. But at the same time, given what we know about our own internal powers of healing, our society can do much more than simply provide an ever-expanding array of technologies and drugs. We can utilize the powers we have, and that means we can engage the connection as part of treatment and care.

It's not that people have forgotten about the human connection. It's just that when they're ill, they fail to consider it as part of their healing tool kit. Most, even when they have a choice, don't seek connectedness as a central component of their treatment. They'll pick high-ranking hospitals and clinics with great reputations (because great reputations are capable of instilling hope). Yet I'm always amazed when I hear patients describe how they're willing to endure doctors with terrible personal skills or clinics where they feel uncomfortable. I've heard people say, "So-and-so surgeon is the best. I want the best doctors in the field. I don't need them to be nice to me." But research reveals, that yes indeed, patients do need their doctors to be nice.[11] And they need them to be engaged, because a physician's compassion helps reduce complications.

WHAT WE SAY AND HOW WE SAY IT

What do I mean by "human connection?" It's fair to say that the definition is bound to vary. In some cases, a connection may simply mean more effective conversations. Studies have looked at that connection—when doctors and patients spend more time talking—and found that it can alter medical care. When patients and doctors have the opportunity to connect with each other, the treatment plan tends to require fewer high-tech diagnostic tests and interventions. One study of one hundred primary care practitioners in Rochester, New York, for instance, found that when doctors took the time to initiate a conversation, establish a positive relationship, and spent longer than usual with each patient, all of the expensive, intrusive aspects of care—from tests to repeat office visits to hospital treatments—were needed less frequently.[12] When an active therapeutic process was initiated, there was less need for passive treatments or diagnostic tests.

I experienced this on a personal level while conducting consults during my integrative medicine fellowship at the University of Arizona. I would first meet with patients to listen to and document their health histories. I asked them to come back two weeks later, after I'd had a chance to research their case so that I could give them a health plan with therapies based on what I'd discovered. That meant I didn't make any therapeutic recommendations until the second visit. Astonishingly, most of the time the patients would return with stories of how good they felt . . . even before I'd prescribed anything!

A more intense level of connection occurs when doctors show higher degrees of caring. Several studies are now looking to quantify the effects of empathy on patient outcomes. Researchers at Sidney Kimmel Medical College at Thomas Jefferson University in Philadelphia, for instance, surveyed doctors about their own ability to be empathetic.[13] These responses were grouped into categories of high, medium, and low empathy scores. The researchers analyzed whether any of the groups were better able to reach their patients with diabetes. Specifically, they wanted to know whether patients of doctors with different degrees of empathy impacted the control their patients had over blood sugar by measuring tests known as the hemoglobin A1c score as well as LDL cholesterol scores, which can be risk factors for heart disease if not properly managed.

The study revealed that people who were seeing doctors with the highest empathy scores were most likely to have good control of their A1c levels because they were more likely to monitor their blood, take medication appropriately, and improve diet and exercise. Those seeing doctors with the lowest empathy scores fared much worse in managing their disease. When it came to the control of cholesterol, which involves making significant lifestyle changes, the differences between the two groups were even more pronounced. Taking into account other statistics—patients' and doctors' ages and genders, as well as socioeconomic factors like health insurance—the researchers concluded that physician empathy played a very significant role in how motivated patients were and how adept they became in managing their own health. Knowing that someone cares helps people help themselves.

LESSONS FROM TREATING THE COMMON COLD

Because I found all of this research compelling, I put the connection to the test in my own clinic at the University of Wisconsin. My colleague and friend Bruce Barrett, a family medicine physician, gifted researcher, and human rights activist, was awarded a large grant to explore the best possible treatment for the common cold. Typical colds are caused by viruses, and even with all of our modern pharmaceuticals, we haven't yet found a highly effective cure. Barrett's study compared a range of treatment approaches, including the herbal remedy echinacea, which was compared to a placebo.[14]

I was particularly interested in whether the quality of

interfaces between clinicians and patients could affect recovery, and I took the lead on a related study that compared the results of different types of physician-patient interactions during office visits. I wanted to explore whether various levels of engagement during a doctor's appointment could alter a cold-sufferer's rate of recovery. To do so, we enrolled 350 patients over the age of twelve with common colds. We found those people by putting out a questionnaire and asking them, quite simply, whether they thought they had a cold. They had to be suffering from the usual symptoms: a runny nose, stuffiness, sneezing, or a sore throat that had started within the previous forty-eight hours.

Then we randomly selected patients to receive one of three types of office visits. A sealed envelope designating what kind of interaction the clinician should conduct was inserted in the patient's chart. In the "no visit" group, the patient did not see medical personnel at all. If the envelope designated that the patient was to have a "standard visit," the doctor or nurse practitioner would carry out a formal, impersonal, if slightly unfriendly, evaluation. But some envelopes would assign a patient to receive an "enhanced visit." In this case, the clinician would embark on engaging the patient in a warm, personal, and highly interactive way.

In fact, we trained our participants with the help of an acting coach who taught several easily reproduced techniques. In the case of the standard visit, clinicians were to have a cool, businesslike, standoffish demeanor and to engage in minimal personal interactions. The coach even suggested that they think of the word "disconnect" before entering the exam room. With the enhanced visit, however, they were trained to think of the word "connection" and aim to establish a bond with the patient during the appointment.

In addition, during the enhanced visit, the clinician would take the time to provide five key elements. For one, the patient would receive a positive prognosis—in other words, be reassured that she would get better soon. Second, the clinician would show empathy and compassion; he fully understood how badly she was feeling. Third, the clinician would give the patient a sense of empowerment over the illness, putting her in control of her own recovery. Fourth, the clinician would make a personal connection with the patient. During the exchange, he would acknowledge that the patient is an individual with a unique history, life circumstances, and worldview, not simply a "case" to deal with or a collection of symptoms to address. Last, the clinician would provide education about the cold and what patients could do therapeutically to recover faster if they chose to. We labeled these steps PEECE, an acronym for *p*ositive prognosis, *e*mpathy, *e*mpowerment, *c*onnection, and *e*ducation.[15]

The clinicians didn't know what type of visit would take place until they opened the envelope just before entering the exam room where the patient was waiting. In the computer-selected, randomized shuffle of names, I sometimes opened standard and other times enhanced-visit envelopes and had to then proceed as directed. Personally, as you'll see in Chapter 3, I found it excruciating to conduct an aloof, formal exam, without smiling or involving the patient at all.[16]

After the office visits, the patients filled out a questionnaire about their appointment. They were asked, on a scale of 1–5, what they thought of various elements of the clinician's behavior and how the behavior made them feel. Did the clinician put them at ease? Did the clinician allow them to tell their own story? Did they feel that the clinician really listened? Was the clinician interested in them as a whole person? Did the clinician have a positive attitude? How well did the clinician understand their concerns, show care and compassion, and explain the illness clearly? And finally, did the clinician help them take control and create a health-based plan of action? A "perfect" encounter resulted in a score of 50.

In the study, 84 of the 350 enrollees gave their clinicians perfect scores. Most of those giving the perfect assessment had received the enhanced visit (although some with a standard visit gave a perfect score, too). But the real measure was to determine whether enhanced visits affected patients' recovery. So, in addition to the survey, our researchers also took biological samples from the participants. With a nasal swab, they were able to measure levels of nasal neutrophils (a white blood cell that fights infection) and an inflammatory cytokine, the protein interleukin 8, which surges as part of the disease-fighting process at the beginning of a viral respiratory infection and then ebbs during the following days to weeks. The presence of neutrophils and IL-8 correlate well with symptoms and can be reliably measured to determine how strenuously the body is fighting the cold.

Following the appointments, surveys, and sample taking, patients went home. During the next two weeks, our researchers called them daily to ask, "Do you think you still have a cold?" At follow-up visits, approximately forty-eight hours after the initial appointment, our researchers remeasured the patients' IL-8 and nasal neutrophil levels.

What we discovered was quite impressive. When we correlated the survey results with the patients' recovery rates, we found that the people who experienced the enhanced visit were the ones whose colds resolved most quickly. In fact, they recovered more than a day sooner than those who had had standard visits. But there was a fascinating finding within those results: The speedier recovery time was strongly associated with those who had rated their enhanced visit a perfect score of 50. There were a scant few who underwent a standard visit, gave the doctor a perfect score, and got well sooner, too. But the most impressive trend was that the first group not only had shorter and less severe colds but their IL-8 and neutrophil measures rose faster to attack the cold virus. The molecular change suggested their bodies were working harder to fight the infection.[17]

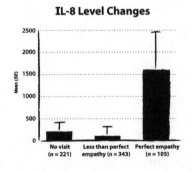

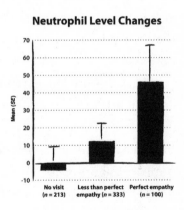

These results provide another peek into how human interactions may have a distinct and measurable physiological effect on the body. Moreover, that effect may be profound enough to kick a person's own disease-fighting mechanisms into high gear. Making a connection may not bring about a cure, but it may prompt better, faster recovery. This is what I mean when I say that a connection can stimulate self-healing mechanisms within a patient's body.

However, the association of the perfect score was of utmost importance. We found that people who experienced an enhanced visit, but gave the clinician a less-than-perfect score, showed little improvement in their recovery time. This provided a fascinating piece of information. We postulated that a perfect score resulted when a "connection" occurred between clinician and patient during the office visit. That connection—something more than "kindness" or "good bedside manner"—may be the necessary condition to really impact another person. In other words, the connection is not merely experiencing someone being nice, but an "on or off" phenomenon. Patients either feel that a person *really hears them* and is *really responding to them* or they don't. When they do, they can gain the emotional and physiological benefits of that interaction.

As a side note, the patients who saw no clinician at all recovered slightly faster than those who underwent a standard visit and rated the doctor low in empathy. This finding affected so small a segment of the participants that it was not deemed of statistical significance. But the tiny quirk in our data made us wonder whether *people may be better off staying home with their dogs than seeing a grumpy doctor who doesn't make the effort to establish a connection!*

Taken together, all of these studies suggest the potential power of the mind in the course of recovery. This is not to say that caregivers can put the burden on people who are sick to gain mental control over their bodies or even that they can always hope their interactions will have the effect they want. Sadly, the mind and body don't always work that way. However, the studies underscore what we've long known. Caregivers, whether professionals or family members, have another approach available to them when serving others. The more they understand the function the mind plays in recovery, the more they can focus on it as a routine element of care. As connected caregivers, they can play as important a role as medications. Indeed, the concerted engagement with another person can provide the first, essential nudge toward healing.

As evidenced in the pages of this book, when caregivers apply a few specific strategies, they can make meaningful connections with others. In these connections, they offer the opportunity for people to feel they are being heard completely, and they create space to feel respected and understood. They affirm that the others' perspective is meaningful, even when it differs from their own. In building trust in that interaction, they can encourage the people they're caring for to bring the most useful information to the conversation, which helps everyone glimpse the big picture. They can then offer their own skills in service of people in need.

LISTENING HELPS CREATE THE CONNECTION

In my circumstance with my complex patient Martha, aware of my frustration and disgusted by my own sense of futility, I took a deep, steadying breath that helped me recall the power of connection and an interactive exchange. I thought about Martha's out-of-control symptoms, how she was navigating one after the next, and the various side effects of the drugs that were supposed to be helping her. The next thought came with utmost clarity. I would not be as helpful to her if I revealed my frustration. Nor would I be effective if I continued on the same course. It occurred to me that perhaps I wasn't the one who should determine which solutions she most needed. She had come to me for help and to give her some answers, but in actuality she would know best what kind of help would feel like a "success" to her.

At that moment, what I had learned from my research on the cold seemed particularly relevant. How could I use all the resources at my disposal—not just medical information, but my presence—to be of help to this person? I could recognize the limits of what I could do for Martha, but I could also appreciate how to be of service most effectively. My best approach wouldn't be to provide answers, but to connect with her in such a way that we would both gain insight into her health. As a clinician, I needed to hear and understand how *she* perceived her illness and what *she* believed she could do to change its course. Importantly, in engaging in a compassionate conversation, I could help her feel in control.

Instead of telling her what I saw in her symptoms or analyzing the latest one, I decided to pose a question. "Martha," I asked, "rheumatoid arthritis has been so hard for you for so long, and it has had so many different and difficult effects. What do you feel is at the bottom of all this?"

To my great surprise, the question opened up a conversation. She told me about how hard her condition had been on her family, and how her inactivity had impinged upon their lives. "I hate to disappoint my son and my husband," she said, "but I don't think they fully understand my constant pain." Then, her eyes welled as she told me about a part of her history I'd never known. Several decades earlier, long before she'd had any symptoms, she had gone through a time of terrible financial distress. In order to support her family, she had briefly prostituted herself. For years, she'd been harboring feelings of shame and remorse about this regrettable period in her life and had told no one. As she cried, I listened. It was a profound moment for me, taking in her emotional release. Her tears provided an insight into the great well of feelings she connected to her sense of being ill. In the conversation, she put words to her desire to get better and also to the negative emotions she felt were hindering that goal. She also linked her disease and its effects on her daily activities to her view of her family that she loved deeply and that gave purpose to her life.

Our conversation didn't present a cure, but it certainly provided a major shift in the course of Martha's treatment. It gave her an opportunity to share various elements of her experience that she was holding inside as "unhealthy." Her disease might have had specific physiological components, but one's emotional state matters, too. In the conversation that evolved between us, she was the one who described the illness, its effects, and its impact on her relationships. I listened, and an important change took place. Suddenly, we had a new framework to discuss her very difficult situation. And we had fresh strategies regarding what she could do to address it. It was a beautiful moment.

Though the rheumatoid arthritis didn't disappear, Martha's overall condition improved considerably following that appointment. As part of her medical treatment, we discussed the merits of her seeking help from a therapist to deal with the unresolved feelings about her past, and she did. She continued to see me for medical treatment of her condition, but over time, her symptoms ceased spiraling out of control, and we were able to decrease several of the medications she was taking. Our connection grew, and we both gained insight about the complexity of emotions, life events, and chronic disease.

For me, the experience with Martha underscored the observation made nearly a century ago by British psychiatrist Henry Maudsley as he linked a person's emotional state to their health: "The sorrow that hath no vent in tears, may make other organs weep." When caregivers help others, particularly those who are suffering, they have more resources at their disposal if they consider a patient's well-being. Martha's situation also showed me that even one brief conversation can have significant results, and that there are ways to have that interaction that can be used strategically to enhance outcomes. Compassionate listening changed the dynamic between me and Martha and set her on a course that not only validated her experiences but also allowed her to design the next steps in her recovery. The conversation may even have inspired her to have hope, which can be a critical boost, especially when problems have persisted for a long time.

The dialogue also changed my perspective of myself as a person who serves others. In place of frustration, it brought about calmness—and also fulfillment. The positive emotions I'd cherished about my career returned. I felt less like I'd done a patch job and more like I'd offered meaningful help, the kind of assistance that could carry Martha into her future. Our interaction recharged my sense of purpose and gave me clarity about my own potential. Although I had imposed myself and my worldview *less* on her situation, I had managed to achieve more.

But even more surprising was the sense of uplift that stirred inside me. The brief connection that Martha and I shared was invigorating. I had more focus and better energy to give to the rest of my day. When I went home that night, I felt that something meaningful had transpired, and I was honored to have been a part of it.

· · ·

Although most of the research in this book is based upon investigations within the medical community, it is applicable to everyone committed to making a connection happen between two people, whether doctor/patient, husband/wife, parent/child, teacher/student, boss/employee, or anyone in a relationship in which one person is charged with supporting another. I have no doubt that people can do their best work—in fact be *of greatest service*—when they focus on the steps of connectedness. The process involves understanding themselves first and being intentional in their presence with others. Making the connection takes practice, but the rewards are palpable. Not only does it foster good health and healing in others, but practitioners of this modality can also recharge their own stores of energy and infuse their experience with a sense of joy.

2

The Mind and the Body—Connected

I find, by experience, that the mind and the body are more than married, for they are most intimately united; and when one suffers, the other sympathizes.

—LORD CHESTERFIELD

The mind is its own place, and in itself can make a Heaven of Hell, a Hell of Heaven.

—JOHN MILTON, *Paradise Lost*

One's expectations are potent arbiters of well-being. But the curious case of Mr. Wright was proof, for the eminent psychologist Bruno Klopfer, that the mind can be so powerful it may even influence a cure. Writing half a century ago, Klopfer was one of the pioneers of the Rorschach test. Among his research interests was the exploration of "psychological variables," including ego and degrees of hopefulness, and how they could help in cancer care. In a talk he gave in 1957, he relayed one patient's experience, as told to him by the patient's doctor, to show how the mind should be recognized as an important tool in treatment.[1]

There was little doubt among the doctors seeing Mr. Wright at a well-known clinic that he had little time left to live. He was suffering with a terrible type of lymphosarcoma that had spread throughout his body. The tumors in his neck, groin, and abdomen were the size of oranges, and radiation treatments would no longer shrink them. He was weak and had even resorted to taking breaths from an oxygen mask. His doctors, agreeing that treatment options had run out, were ready to provide palliative care until he succumbed to the disease.

But Mr. Wright seemed to have lucky timing. Just as doctors were conferring about his imminent end, a new drug came on the market, a chemical derived from a horse serum. Enthusiasm about the drug, known as Krebiozen, was rampant. Even the newspapers were reporting that it was a miraculous cancer cure. Mr. Wright read the accounts and found out that the clinic where he was being treated was one of the few test sites for the drug. He wanted to join the study. At first, his doctor resisted. He didn't believe Mr. Wright, who seemed unlikely to live for more than two weeks, would qualify for the drug trial, which stipulated at least a three-month life expectancy. But Mr. Wright was absolutely certain that the miracle drug would make a difference and begged to receive it.

Mr. Wright's case involves several deviations from ethics protocols that wouldn't be allowed today, such as his doctor including him in a clinical trial simply on grounds of sympathy.

But those deviations paved the way for some truly remarkable results. Mr. Wright received his first injections of Krebiozen on a Friday. His doctor returned on Monday to find his patient not only in excellent spirits and chatting energetically with the hospital staff, but with shrinking tumors. Astounded, the physician proceeded to give Mr. Wright the full course of treatment. Within ten days, he no longer appeared to be dying. He was breathing on his own and was so full of energy that the doctors decided to discharge him from the hospital.

However, over the course of the next two months, conflicting reports about the effectiveness of Krebiozen began to appear in newspapers. Many challenged the original research, and new information appeared that the drug was a sham. Mr. Wright, who'd kept up on the reports, was devastated by the news. He relapsed after two healthy months and returned to the hospital in a dismal state.

Recognizing that Mr. Wright's hopefulness might have played a role in his two-month recovery, his physician decided to engage his positive outlook. Today's ethics standards would never permit what happened next, but the doctor, having nothing more to offer his patient, told Mr. Wright that a new, double-strength preparation of the drug was arriving at the hospital, and that Mr. Wright was eligible to receive it. Even though he gave Mr. Wright nothing but fresh water injections, the doctor gave every indication that he was hopeful about the enhanced Krebiozen.

Mr. Wright's enthusiasm returned, and the results were even more astounding than they'd been the first time. The tumors shrank again, his energy returned, and he was discharged from the hospital a second time. In fact, his health lasted two more months—until a definitive medical report appeared from the American Medical Association, stating that Krebiozen was a "worthless" drug. The news rattled Mr. Wright. Within a week of the public report, he was rehospitalized and died two short days later.

For Klopfer, who recounted the story in an address to a psychological professional society, the unusual case suggested that certain "types" of patients have a better opportunity to heal. Those individuals with fewer emotional impediments— less fear and more hope—are ultimately better equipped. Mr. Wright's positive spirit "left all available vital energy free to produce a response to the cancer treatment that was nothing short of miraculous," Klopfer wrote. The results didn't last, he added, because the patient was easily swayed by disappointment, but the relationship with his doctor—and his doctor's enthusiasm for the treatment—clearly affected his survival.

While this case provides an interesting narrative, it also raises some important questions: *What if we learned to pay more attention to features like optimism? What if clinicians were trained to consider patients' emotional capabilities as part of treatment?* and *What exactly is the connection between the mind and healing?*

ENGAGING THE MIND FOR THE SAKE OF THE BODY

One of the long-standing characteristics of Western medicine, dating to the writings of Descartes in the eighteenth century, has been the dualistic separation of mind and body. The reductionist approach (referred to as the Cartesian split, and understood to be *either* body or mind, one or the other) has shaped how we as a society treat disease, how we approach research, and how we talk with people needing care. Health care systems have been structured along those lines, too. It is a zero-sum game. No one is surprised to learn that a friend with a heart problem will visit a cardiologist, and a different friend with cancer will see an oncologist. But people expect that their friends' emotional, spiritual, and relational needs will be addressed elsewhere—with some other type of mental health clinician or counselor, if at all—but not in the specialized medical suite.

However, the exciting news is that our society is becoming increasingly comfortable entertaining the idea of the interconnectedness of mind and body. Wide-ranging randomized clinical studies from molecular biology to social sciences and a great deal of scientific evidence support the idea that both are integrally involved in sickness and recovery and that an individual's emotional experience and expectations play a large role as well.[2] When people perceive information with their minds, it triggers the creation of a protein in the brain (a neuropeptide) that starts a cascade of physiological reactions that travel throughout the physical body. So, to be 100 percent accurate, no one would ever separate the mind from the body. Taken together, they are one interactive whole. Current research is helping us understand the fluid connection between the two— we cannot influence one without affecting the other. As naturalist John Muir has said, "When we try to pick out anything by itself, we find it hitched to everything else in the Universe."[3]

The fact is, we know that personal interactions can make

a difference in healing. Randomized clinical studies into the mind/body connection are important, because in addition to living in an era of technological advances, we're also in an age that prizes what's known as "evidence-based medicine." This strives for treatments that include clinician insight and "the best available external clinical evidence from systematic research."[4] In short, if we are going to stand by any type of care, train people to administer it, and implement it in a rigorous way, we want scientific proof that it works. This is all for the good.

Evidence-based mind/body studies are showing that despite all the drugs and technologies at our disposal, our emotional experience during an illness matters as much today as it did centuries ago. For instance, seminal mind/body research at Stanford University as far back as the 1980s found that women with metastatic breast cancer had longer survival rates when they were active participants in support groups that enabled them to express their emotions.[5] The latest research in this field by Barbara Andersen at The Ohio State University confirms that the active treatment involved in group support can lengthen lives.[6] In this more recent investigation, 227 women with breast cancer were divided into groups that either did or did not participate in support groups of eight to twelve patients. During the sessions, two clinical psychologist leaders conducted interventions like relaxation training as well as discussions about positive ways to cope with cancer-related stress and fatigue, how to increase social support, healthy strategies to improve diet and exercise regimens, and adherence to cancer treatments. The women participated in twenty-six sessions spread over twelve months.

Then, all of the patients (those in the groups as well as the controls who did not participate) were followed for eleven years, during which time sixty-two had a recurrence of cancer. Of these sixty-two, some dropped out of the study or were too ill to participate. Ultimately, forty-one of the women with metastatic cancer were evaluated at intervals of four, eight, and twelve months. They were assessed for their psychological state, social networks, adherence to medical protocols, and immune system function (including the strength of their natural killer cells and the proliferation of T cells, a type of lymphocyte or white blood cell that plays a central role in immunity).

Dr. Andersen and her team found that the women who had participated in the support groups enjoyed biobehavioral advantages and as a consequence had a lower risk of death and a longer life span after their cancer recurred than those who had not participated in the groups. In addition, there was a longer interval between the initial diagnosis and the recurrence— affording these women more time to live cancer-free. These positive effects may have arisen from many different sources, including feeling part of a community of support, reduced anxiety and depression, and having the opportunity to express emotions about the disease.

This mind/body study is now considered the final word on the subject—and it points to the power of the human connection in healing and even in longevity. In fact, the Institute of Medicine of the National Academy of Sciences[7] recommended the inclusion of these kinds of psychosocial peer support groups as part of the gold standard for the treatment of cancer. In their report *Cancer Care for the Whole Patient: Meeting Psychosocial Health Needs*, the Institute stated: "Evidence emerging from the science of psychoneuroimmunology—the study of the inter-actions among behavior, the brain, and the body's immune system—is beginning to show how psychosocial stressors inter-fere with the working of the body's neuro-endocrine, immune, and other systems." One of the recommended approaches to mitigating the pernicious effects of the negative emotions accompanying the illness and its treatments are peer support groups. Indeed, the Institute also made a case for a strength-ened connection between patients and those caring for them: "All cancer care should ensure the provision of psychosocial health services by facilitating *effective communication* between patients and care providers."[8]

ACTIVE VERSUS PASSIVE TREATMENTS

Why did the women in Barbara Andersen's cancer support groups benefit from their participation? Some of the potential emotional consequences of cancer diagnosis and treatment include depression, anxiety, and posttraumatic stress disorder. People struggling with these emotional issues along with the disease may have difficulty adhering to the treatments their doctors recommend, which could shorten their life spans. In addition, they may suffer from pain, insomnia, and fatigue that could impact their ability to continue working (and earn-ing a living) and carrying out their normal roles in life. All of these issues can compound their depression and worsen their health outcomes.

I believe that one of the reasons the support group extended lives is that regular psychosocial meetings such as those conducted at The Ohio State University or in other institutions such as the Cancer Support Community are *active* treatments. Rather than being passive victims of their disease and its difficult treatments and side effects, patients in support groups become engaged in their own fight for recovery.[9] From my years of experience (and with increasingly convincing evidence from ongoing research in the field), I have found that healing requires just such an active process. It occurs when the people needing help form a strong connection to those who seek to help them.

Moreover, I have found that a connected interaction may be far more beneficial and far less harmful than quickly prescribing drugs—a much more passive approach. For one thing, as I mentioned earlier, drug interactions and polypharmacy cause far too many problems. For example, dementia or memory loss are common concerns, particularly as people age. Physicians generally prescribe medications with acetyl-cholinesterase inhibitors (like Aricept) to treat these conditions because they increase acetyl-choline, the neurotransmitter needed to make memories. However, other treatments with side effects that lower acetyl-choline are often prescribed simultaneously. These medications (many ending in "ine") are used for allergies (Benadryl or diphenhydramine and Claritin or loratadine); muscle spasms (Detrol or tolterodine for bladder control); and depression, pain, and insomnia (Cymbalta or duloxetine and Elavil or amitriptyline) to name just a few. All of them have now been found to increase the risk of memory loss if used long term because they inhibit acetyl-choline, the very neurotransmitter that helps make memories.[10] So one drug interferes with the action of the other—leading to poorer outcomes and frustration all around.

Besides, simply prescribing a pill does not require caregivers or patients to interact as they contemplate how life circumstances may have affected health, which I believe is a central element to healing. Let's look at depression as a prime example of the potential dangers involved in a passive methodology. This disease has many origins (including life circumstances, genetics, and other illnesses such as cancer, hypothyroidism, and Parkinson's) that can exacerbate symptoms. One of its underlying physiological causes is a lessened amount of serotonin, the feel-good hormone, in the brain. Selective serotonin reuptake inhibitor (SSRI) antidepressants, such as Prozac or Zoloft, work because they block receptors for this hormone, thus allowing more of it to circulate where it's needed. Since the development of SSRIs, doctors have been treating depression passively with these drugs for many years now. In fact, taking pills, receiving acupuncture, or getting a massage are all *passive* therapies.

However, for every action there is a reaction. In the case of treatment with SSRIs, a less favorable result, called oppositional tolerance, can develop.[11] When the medication artificially blocks serotonin receptors with an SSRI, the body listens and adapts. Thinking it needs more receptors for serotonin, it creates them. Over time, a patient may develop tolerance to the antidepressant; since the body has boosted the number of serotonin receptors, the dose needs to increase too, in order to have the same "feel good" effect.

But let's say a person doesn't like the sexual side effects of the antidepressant. Or his mood is improving, and he feels he no longer needs the drug. So he stops cold turkey. Now the serotonin receptors are no longer blocked, which means that he has many more than he did before starting the medication. As a result, circulating serotonin binds to all these newly formed receptors, which triggers their levels to drop drastically—like water running down an open drain. This causes the person to feel terrible—even more depressed than before. He believes that he really needs to go back on the SSRI. The key, therefore, is to stop taking the drug gradually, so the body can readapt to a lower dose over time.

This same process occurs with many other medications and procedures. For instance, if doctors prescribe opioids like hydrocodone or morphine for pain, when all the opioid receptors are bound with the medication, the body adapts and creates more of them. Over time, treatment with opioids can increase pain sensitivity in some people, actually worsening the very problem we are trying to resolve. This is known in the literature as opioid-induced hyperalgesia.[12]

Similarly, when we shut off the acid pump in the stomach for extended periods of time with proton pump inhibitors such as Prilosec, the body thinks it needs to make more acid and is primed to do so—like a horse ready to bolt out of the gate at the Kentucky Derby. When the drug is stopped, the acid levels rise higher than usual (in a process called rebound hyperacidity), and patients develop severe acid reflux symptoms. Studies have found that physicians can actually cause heartburn in people who never had it before if they put them on acid-suppressing drugs for at least six weeks and then stop them abruptly.[13] Not only that, recent research has shown that shutting off the acid pump long term with these drugs also causes nutrient malabsorption and increases the risk of dementia, heart disease, and kidney disease.[14] There can be long-term harm from overuse of this quick fix. On the other hand, if a patient considers the metaphor "What's eating me up inside?" maybe he won't need to simply turn to a drug to block the acid pump.

Major bariatric surgery for obesity also leads to oppositional tolerance. The most successful form of this surgery is called a Roux-en-Y. The stomach is bypassed by replumbing the gastrointestinal track. A pouch that holds only a cup of food is fashioned from the small intestine. This is then attached to where the stomach used to be. The stomach is still present (it allows pancreatic enzymes to continue to digest food), but it's off on its own now, creating the left side of the *Y*. Successful surgery can result in significant weight loss and even reversal of diabetes. But if a person regains her appetite and returns to consuming the same large meals, the body adapts. The one-cup pouch stretches to the size of the original stomach, and the pounds pile back on. In fact, after five years, 50 percent of people return to their original weight, with the addition of a number of side effects related to this aggressive surgery.[15] This setback might have been prevented had the patient and clinician explored the emotional reasons behind the overeating.

The human body, and all of life for that matter, is remarkably adaptive. It has tremendous potential to heal if we take the time and attention to help it along. In Buddhist philosophy, there is a saying that encourages us not to "push the river." When we try to change the normal course of nature, the river may overflow its banks, causing harm. Medications have been, and still remain, one of the most valuable therapeutic tools we have to treat disease, but if we overuse them and do not address concomitant emotional issues, we can "push the river" of the body.

There is another way. Indeed, healing from within requires a connection with another human being to develop insight into the real, underlying cause that may be triggering the body to react with symptoms. So if someone is depressed and bonds with a therapist who helps him understand what initiated his despair and how he can change his life, he then develops insight into the problem instead of simply manipulating serotonin receptors. This is why research shows that cognitive behavioral therapy (also known as CBT; reflecting on one's situation, learning, and making changes) works as well as medication and with fewer relapses.[16] This approach encourages exploration of situations that have led to patterns of behavior. Self-examination results in insights into how to proactively change the course of one's life. Active therapies sustain healing. Passive therapies, like antidepressants, proton pump inhibitors, and bariatric surgery, can help reduce symptoms but they are not as sustaining, and often unsustainable.

Just taking the medicine without insight rarely results in healing. We are more effective when people can actively mobilize the body's and mind's own resources. But this requires caregivers and patients alike to turn toward challenges and suffering, which is much harder than simply taking a pill. Often both pills and behavioral therapy are needed and many people stay on medications long term. But for those with mild to moderate depression, I use these medicines only short term to improve energy and mood sufficiently to empower my patients to work on the active treatments. And then, if possible, I taper off the medication before oppositional tolerance develops.

Other active therapies have also been found to be quite powerful—for example, mindfulness, an ancient Buddhist practice, is the process of living in the present moment, on purpose, without judgment (see Chapter 7). Most of the time, the mind dwells in memories of the past or in the desires or expectations of the future. Most stressful thoughts come from past regrets— the "I should (and shouldn't) haves" (*I should have stopped at that red light. I should have asked her out on a date. I shouldn't have sold that stock!*) and fears for the future—the "what ifs" (*What if I don't pass this test? What if this relationship doesn't work out? What if my child gets hurt at camp?*). Regret traps the mind in the past and anxiety traps the mind in the future. Purposefully living in the present moment gets people out of the past and the future (about which they can do nothing) and into the "what *is*." And research has shown that mindfulness-based cognitive therapy (MBCT),[17] achieved through carefully structured meditations on the present moment, can reduce stress, anxiety, insomnia, pain, and depression.[18] A positive experience can boost treatment and even provide better outcomes.

Jon Kabat-Zinn, a pioneer in bringing mindfulness practice from the East to the West, found that this meditation technique even improved the symptoms of a physical ailment such as psoriasis. The patients in his research were undergoing treatment of their red, scaly lesions using ultraviolet phototherapy, but those who also meditated using mindful techniques found their skin cleared up faster than those who did not.[19]

Whether caregivers are treating patients or helping a loved one recover, they can put the mind's capabilities to work in healing. And one of the very best ways to boost good, positive, optimistic feelings is through a human connection that elicits hope and the expectation of a positive outcome.

THE SO-CALLED PLACEBO EFFECT

One of my patients, an ultramarathoner who runs one hundred-mile races, told me something that has stuck with me: "The mind always goes before the legs." To run one hundred miles, both the body and the mind need to be fit, but the mind is in control. Beliefs about what is or isn't possible send more or less energy to the muscles to do the job. The mind pulls the levers that make the body keep going, even under these extreme conditions. The relationship between mind and body continues to be a surprise to people, but it shouldn't be. What we think and what we expect can change the course of the body's responses. And this is particularly true of what we have come to call placebos.

In 1807, Thomas Jefferson wrote, "One of the most successful physicians I have ever known has assured me that he used more bread pills, drops of colored water, and powders of hickory ashes, than of all other medicines put together."[20]

Placebos! In Latin, the term means "I shall please." The placebo effect refers to a patient's positive belief that a treatment will work—and often it does. Many experiments have shown that placebos can play a role in improving asthma, heart problems, and even kidney disease. For instance, it has been found that blue placebo pills are more sedating than pink, and red ones are more effective than beige. Placebo pills that are "branded" are more helpful than generics. Bigger pills are "stronger" than smaller ones, and on and on.[21] In fact, the more an intervention hurts, the stronger the placebo effect. Moreover, a recent research study has shown that the context of how the placebo therapy is administered (in this case, to people who suffered from osteoarthritis in the knee) influenced outcomes. As expected, the doctor giving a placebo shot or rubbing on a cream relieved pain more effectively than when patients simply were given a capsule to swallow.[22]

Outcomes such as these are emblematic of the power of engaging a person's own healing mechanisms. Call it the "placebo effect" if you will, but this is more than simply giving a dummy pill. In fact, I feel the term "placebo effect" can be misleading since it may suggest trickery. I believe a better term would be "the healing effect."

The mind's influence is especially powerful when it comes to the body's self-healing capacity. Also known as "interpersonal healing," it is initiated by the interaction between doctor and patient. It can be triggered by many behaviors, symbols, and rituals in the clinical encounter, all of which provide a patient with hope, trust, meaning, support, and empathy.[23] Indeed, placebos have dramatic potential to propel healing when caregivers are able to create the ideal belief, expectancy, and ceremony to trigger these mechanisms. They are beneficial in their own right if used strategically by a gifted clinician.

For instance, in 2006, Bruce Wampold and his team of researchers at the University of Wisconsin published their findings after analyzing the data from a 1985 landmark study by the National Institute of Mental Health (NIMH). The latter stressed the benefit of the antidepressant imipramine over a placebo. The Wisconsin team was concerned that this original investigation did not take into account the impact of the clinician prescribing the drug so they looked at 112 patients more closely to determine whether the psychiatrist–patient relationship had influenced the outcomes. They found that psychiatrists who were good at developing rapport and a trusting relationship had better results with a sugar pill than psychiatrists less skillful in these techniques when they prescribed the *active drug*. They also showed that this "talented" group had even better outcomes when they used the active drug. The connection the psychiatrists made with their patients was more powerful than the medication. And when they used the real medicine, the healing effect was enhanced.[24]

Even more interestingly, a new study conducted in Portugal has shown that placebos are more effective for lower back pain than traditional treatments even when patients are told in advance that they are taking an inert compound. The rationale for this study: No single treatment has yet been found to significantly decrease pain when used alone. One of the most common medications given for back pain—nonsteroidal anti-inflammatory drugs (NSAIDs) such as Advil or Aleve or the more potent prescription versions—reduces pain but only by about 1 point on the 10-point pain scale.[25] And contrary to popular belief, opioids are also anemic pain relievers as they have not been found to significantly benefit pain, function, or quality of life over the long term.[26] So if the intrinsic value of the medication doesn't do much, scientists have proposed that maybe physicians could create ceremony, ritual, and positive expectations to enhance outcomes. That's exactly what researchers did in Portugal.

They randomly divided eighty-three people with low back pain into two groups. For three months, forty-one of the study participants took an open-label placebo—that is, the label on the pill bottle actually read "Placebo Pills." The other forty-two patients continued treatment as usual without the placebo pills. But the researchers created positive expectations for the placebo pills. All participants were shown a short video summarizing past research supporting positive benefits of open-label placebos, and they were also told the following: "The placebo effect can be powerful. The body's reaction to placebo is similar to the well-known conditioned responses of Pavlov's dogs. A positive attitude can be helpful. Taking the pills faithfully for 21 days is critical." After everyone received this education, they opened the randomized envelopes and those in the research group were given a bottle that was labeled "Placebo Pills. Take 2 twice a day."

The researchers were looking for improvements in pain (on a scale of 1–10) and disability (on a scale of 0–24). They measured these at baseline, before the drugs were taken, and also after eleven and twenty-one days. They found that compared with the 1-point improvement with NSAIDs and a 0.2-point improvement with treatment as usual, the people taking the open-label placebos experienced a 1.5-point reduction of pain. The placebos were even more powerful for disability, which was reduced by 2.9 points on a 24-point scale compared with no improvement at all with the usual treatment regimen.[27]

What are we to take away from this study? I believe that the benefits of any therapy a physician prescribes derives from much more than the intrinsic value of the substance itself. The ritual and expectations created around the medication can enhance its effects. Possessing a bottle labeled "Placebo Pills," opening it, and taking it with the expectancy that even sugar pills can be beneficial, can improve outcomes. In fact, a talented clinician prescribing an open-label placebo can do more good with less harm than someone who doesn't take the time to create positive expectations and prescribes drugs such as NSAIDs and opioids that have well-known and pernicious side effects.

HOW DO PLACEBOS WORK?

These powerful results have been correlated to visible changes in the brain. A person's expectations of improvement stimulate production of dopamine (the reward hormone) and opioids (the pleasure and pain-relieving hormones) and a cascade of other neurotransmitters in the parts of the brain that receive information, process it, and influence emotions. Positron emission tomography (PET) scans light up the parts of the brain that are most active and show that a positive expectation influences the production of dopamine and opioids in the anterior cingulate, orbitofrontal, and insular cortices as well as the nucleus accumbens, amygdala (a small, almond-shaped structure in the brain that mediates emotions), and periaqueductal gray matter. That is strong medicine from a mere thought—an expectation.[28]

One investigation, conducted by researchers from Wake

Forest University and published in the prestigious journal *Proceedings of the National Academy of Sciences,* used functional MRI (fMRI) studies to measure pain and pain relief. The researchers found that when participants subjected to painful patches on their legs were told that their discomfort would be decreased (whether or not it was), they actually reported feeling less pain—28.4 percent less, to be exact. But there was physiological evidence, too: The fMRI scan showed a significant decrease in activity in all pain-centric regions of the brain. In fact, the authors wrote, "positive expectations (that is, expectations for reduced pain) produce a reduction in perceived pain that rivals a clearly analgesic dose of the opioid morphine."[29] The amount of morphine needed to reduce pain by 25 percent is normally 0.08 mg per kilogram of body weight. If a person weighs 170 pounds (77 kg), the positive expectation of reduced pain would have the same effect as if he took 6 mg of morphine. This echoes the findings in the study we discussed in Chapter 1 in which the nurse rather than the computer behind the screen administered the pain medication. In that study, human involvement reduced pain by about 8 mg of morphine.

Nevertheless, as a culture, we take so little stock in placebos because they have been thought of as a sham. They are utilized in clinical trials to gauge the worthiness of an up-and-coming drug. If the experimental chemical outperforms the placebo, which is usually a sugar pill, it's deemed an effective medication and is readied for market. If the placebo is just as or more successful, the new medication is considered ineffectual and is shelved. I will be taking issue with this perception throughout this book. From my experience, interpersonal healing as mediated by the connection is not trickery but a valid and proven modality that modern science is just beginning to capitalize on.

Caregivers possess great potential as healers. They can be far more effective helping others if they take stock of their own powers. They may not be able to enact a cure in patients or loved ones, but they can certainly use their *presence* to mobilize the other person's self-healing resources. They can provide support, a positive outlook, motivation, and hope, which can improve the potential to heal and the eventual outcome. These are the skills of emotional intelligence. When put to good use, caregivers will be able to apply their positive communications in order to set into motion the health of others. In fact, there is a biological root to human connectedness and compassion, one that we will explore in greater depth.

3

The Biology of Connection

All things are connected, like the blood which unites
  one family
All things are connected.
Whatever befalls the earth befalls the sons of the earth.
Man did not weave the web of life, he is merely a strand
  in it.
Whatever he does to the web, he does to himself.

—CHIEF SEATTLE, 1854

It was a routine day during our research study at the University of Wisconsin Hospital and Clinics. We were investigating the differential effects of caregiver empathy versus caregiver aloofness on people with common colds. With instructions for a "standard" (nonempathic) visit in hand, I stepped into an examination room, only to find a twelve-year-old girl waiting there for me. Careful to follow the study's protocol and my assigned role as a detached but efficient clinician, I tried to avoid making eye contact with this young person who was known to me only as case number 406. According to the rules, I had to maintain a disconnected, cool demeanor.

"What brings you in?" I asked as I glanced down at my papers, distancing myself as best I could. I turned my back on her and washed my hands. Of course, I knew why she was in the office. She'd been directed to the research group. But I kept that to myself. I faced her again.

"I have a cold," said the girl, trying to look me in the eye. I sensed her disappointment that I was not returning her inviting gaze. And despite my own need to connect, I kept to the business at hand. "Let's have a look," I said.

She climbed onto the table. Sticking to the "standard" protocol that had been randomly assigned to her case, I remained stony-faced and asked only yes-and-no questions: "Do you have a sore throat?" "Is your nose stuffy?" "Are you sneezing?" I continued avoiding eye contact and successfully dodged the bonding that she eagerly tried to establish, again turning my back to her to make some notes in her chart. Then, without another word, I walked over to the table, examined her throat and ears, pressed on the glands in her neck, and listened for congestion in her lungs. The study coordinator had already swabbed her nose, looking for neutrophils, as our research required.

Fighting the urge to look into her eyes, I ended the visit with the customary phrase, "Do you have any questions?"

"Yes," she said, nodding her head. "Do you have a family?"

This bothered me; I could feel my heart sink. She was reaching out, trying to connect, but I did my duty and stuck to the protocol. Responding in a deadpan monotone, I said, "Yes, a wife and three children." I then cut off any chance for her to respond by following up with, "Anything else?"

She shook her head dejectedly and cast down her eyes.

I wanted to spend more time getting to know her, but I had just quashed any potential for that. She was trying to make a connection, to see what could be, and I failed her.

I left the room as abruptly as I'd come in and hit the "stop" button on my timer: three minutes, eleven seconds. My stomach churned, and I felt nauseated. I became undone in a mere three minutes because I had blocked the friendly signals that a kindhearted child had offered. The potential consequences of my actions made me physically ill. *Did my forced aloofness hurt her as much as it did me? Will it worsen her cold? How will this encounter inform her mind-set about doctors in the future? And will that affect her long-term health?* The statisticians may enjoy finding significance for the "standard" or "enhanced" visits, but at that moment, what was most important to me was how terrible I felt interfering with my patient's attempts to relate to me meaningfully. Even if our research eventually showed that there was no difference in outcome between standard and enhanced interactions, intuitively I knew that creating connections is what helps me facilitate healing and also helps me to feel healthy.

But the bigger question for me was this: *I could see that this engaging girl felt unhappy as a result of our sterile encounter, but why was I so perturbed by it?* After all, I was following a research protocol that our team at the University of Wisconsin had designed. *Was I feeling dejected, the way that she seemed to be feeling? Had I picked up on her emotions? Is there a neurological root to human connectedness?*

HOW OUR NERVOUS SYSTEM SHARES FEELINGS WITH OTHERS

The short answer to these questions is a surprising "Yes."

Bystanders become traumatized when witnessing a car accident or a war atrocity, even if they aren't involved. Grandparents' stomachs drop when they watch their grandchildren clamber to the top of a jungle gym. A baby starts to cry in the backseat of the car when his parents are arguing in the front. And someone like former President Bill Clinton can say, "I feel your pain," and really mean it. These are all examples of how our nervous systems are interconnected and not discrete.

Research shows that from birth onward, on a neurological level, people are quite affected by and absorb the feelings of those around them. That's the basis of empathy, compassion, and learning. These findings lead to the conclusion that in some ways (which most people can't detect), their bodies and brains are physiologically attuned to the people around them. And this connection is even stronger when they take the time to create a bond.

In a famous, although controversial series of studies, researchers took seven pairs of individuals who were strangers to each other and attached them to an electroencephalogram (EEG), a device that senses electrical stimuli in the brain. In the first experiment, the individuals of each pair were kept separate from each other. They were then put into individual cubicles (A and B) called Faraday boxes that block out all electromagnetic waves, which the EEG would detect as brain activity. The person in box A was stimulated by a strobe light and his brain waves were tracked. Then the researchers wanted to see whether they could pick up similar brain waves in the person in box B, even though he sat in darkness. As one might expect, the brain waves of the person in box B were unaltered.

The scientists then changed the experiment. They asked the dyads to get to know each other and "feel each other in meditative silence for 20 minutes." After establishing this kind of intuitive connection, they separated the pair into their respective A and B Faraday boxes and asked them to maintain that feeling of connection. Then they flashed the light into box A. In 25 percent of the cases, which is statistically significant, when the strobe light stimulated the brain of the person in box A, a similar brain wave pattern was detected in the person sitting in box B, even though he was in an environment that prevented him from seeing or otherwise experiencing the light.[1] This is the science of distant intentionality. The researchers were studying the effect of one person on another over distance. For example, if an identical twin can sense that something is wrong with her sibling when she is in Colorado and her sister is in Massachusetts, that would constitute intentionality over distance.

In a follow-up study nine years later, eleven pairs of people who "felt close with an empathic connection" were used to study the potential of distant intentionality. The researchers wanted to determine whether the thoughts of one person could impact the brain activity of another. Working with native Hawaiian healers (who had practiced healing traditions for an average of twenty-three years), they put the "healer" in an electromagnetically sealed room while his or her connected counterpart was slid into an fMRI machine that lights up specific, activated areas of the brain. The healers were told to turn on and off their intention of positive regard at random, unpredictable two-minute intervals to see whether this would correlate with activity registering in their partner's brain on the fMRI. Imagine parents sending loving thoughts to their son or daughter lying calmly in a scanner. Although the recipients did not feel anything, there was a consistent correlation between the distant intentions from the healer and their close comrade in the scanner. The fMRI showed a connection between the brains of the receivers and the thoughtful intentions of the givers that was statistically significant.[2]

This effect is directly related to the strength of the connection. It is more likely to occur if people care for each other. It is also more likely to occur if we take cells that arise from the same living organism and then divide and study their reactions. In Milan, Italy, for instance, Rita Pizzi and her colleagues separated human neurons into two shielded boxes. When a laser light stimulated the neurons in one box, the distant cells in the other box registered the same reaction.[3] Another lab run by Ashkan Farhadi at Rush University in Chicago showed similar results. Dr. Farhadi and his colleagues took epithelial cells that line the gut and separated them in a shielded way that would prevent communication. When the cells in the first box were negatively influenced by toxic hydrogen peroxide, the cells in the second box (which were not exposed to the chemical) were similarly damaged.[4] This study can give us insight into the power of a "gut feeling."

Although physicists try to explain these phenomena through quantum mechanics and complicated hypotheses such as entanglement, it will likely be a while before they figure out how this works. But it does give researchers a way of conceiving how a mother's intuition can perceive whether her child is unhappy. Unfortunately, the negative emotions are often more powerful than the positive ones.

These investigations show how brains may connect to other brains, but what about the heart? At the Institute of HeartMath, widely publicized research has shown that the beating heart, which gives off a certain amount of electromagnetic energy as measured on an electrocardiogram (ECG), resonates within others' brains and elsewhere in their bodies—especially if people are in close proximity to each other or are touching.[5] This is also true for mothers holding their infants as well as a couple sleeping together. In fact, other studies have shown that the closer a married couple synchronizes physiological systems such as heart rate, pulse, skin conductance (an indirect measure of anxiety), and body movements in a phenomenon called coregulation, the more likely they are to report marital satisfaction, and the healthier they tend to be.[6]

This kind of connection goes beyond simple electrical impulses. Attunement and coregulation change the body so that the physiology of one person aligns with what he or she is seeing and feeling in others. For instance, after a group of 132 college students watched a film of Mother Teresa ministering to abandoned, dying children and lepers, the students' immune function (as measured by the level of antibodies in their saliva) improved and stayed at an elevated level for at least an hour. According to the researchers who undertook this intriguing study, during that hour, the students were asked to continue dwelling on personal loving relationships such as those characterized in the film.[7] Simply observing someone creating a connection and holding that in mind has a positive effect on one's body and health.

Others have found that physiological responses influence those of others during social interactions—even if the people are strangers to one another. For instance, research has revealed that feeling cold is actually "contagious." In one study, participants watched videos that depicted actors placing their right or left hand into buckets of warm or icy water. In a phenomenon called somatic simulation, the participants' own hands became significantly colder when they watched the actors plunge their hands into the cold water.[8]

THE ROLE OF MIRROR NEURONS

How are these reactions possible? After all, the students weren't personally benefiting from Mother Teresa's kindnesses. The research subjects didn't put their hands in the cold water—they only watched other people who did. To answer that question, we have to look to scientists who have recently identified what are called "mirror neurons" in the brain. These specialized cells fire in response to individuals' observation of others' intentional actions, thereby evoking the same sensations in themselves. This kind of shared activation and the simulated responses in the brain constitute a biological basis for how to understand what's going on in another person's mind[9]—and is likely fundamental to learning by imitation and, by extension, to human survival as a species since our earliest learning is based on emulating behaviors. (Think of babies mimicking their parent's tongue thrusts and the subtle mouth movements that are observed when a parent talks to them.)

Mirror neurons have always existed, but they were first recognized in 1992 by chance at a lab in Parma, Italy. A team of scientists there had prepared a chimpanzee for brain research, implanting thin probes in the regions known for planning and executing movements. They connected the wires leading from the probes to a computer that would determine which neurons fired when the chimp grabbed a nut or banana. The scientists went about their business, but when one of them started placing food pellets in a box, he happened to glance at the computer screen. There he was astonished to see that the monitor attached to the wires indicated that the chimp had moved, when in fact, it hadn't so much as twitched a muscle. The animal had simply observed the scientist. Even though it remained motionless, the same brain circuits that would have been activated had the chimp grabbed the pellets itself were firing.[10]

This unexpected finding spawned a new arena of research on mirror neurons, which has proceeded from the study of other primates to humans. It is now well established that when people observe others' facial expressions, their faces move in the same ways, though often quite subtly. (By contrast, when they are prevented from mimicking the expression, they are less apt to understand the emotions they're observing.) In France, scientists have been studying the brain patterns that underlie what they call interactional synchrony: During social exchanges, both participants alter their own actions in response to their partner's continuously shifting behavior.[11] In effect, brains become synchronized and through this process, important information is exchanged and a sense of trust is developed. However, lately this important process is being disrupted by technology. As electronic health records become a central part of the patient encounter, the computer screen is drawing more and more attention. The same occurs with smartphones as teenagers increasingly interact with this nonemotional object rather than have face-to-face encounters with their friends. This reliance on computers large and small creates a barrier that prevents interactional synchrony from developing. This conditioning will likely reduce our children's emotional intelligence and intuition.

Research has also moved beyond the understanding that people mirror others' movements to the discovery that they also mirror emotions. Mirror neurons exist in the emotional centers of the brain such as the amygdala. This means that feelings are contagious. The structures involved in their integration and control respond not only to direct stimulation—for example, the pleasure experienced at seeing a close friend—but also to the observation of those emotions in others.[12] This permits people to understand firsthand what someone else is experiencing . . . to literally feel their physical and/or emotional pain. Mirror neurons underlie our capacity to have empathy and compassion for another.[13] Conversely, studies show that when an observer notices her listener isn't mirroring her expressions or having appropriate responses, trust declines.[14]

Of course, this can work in both directions—people pick up on the feelings of those around them—positive or negative, perhaps giving proof to the aphorism: "A family is only as happy as its unhappiest member." Emotional contagion is a well-known, deleterious phenomenon in which mass hysteria can grip a group of people, causing them to believe erroneously that they are in mortal danger or that they have spontaneously developed the same ailment.

The good news here is that sensitized mirror neurons can be cultivated and activated to communicate positive feelings, too. The more people get out of their own clutter (a concept I'll explain in Chapter 6), the more powerfully their mirror neurons will work to connect them to the emotions of those whom they seek to help. Positive emotions are contagious.[15] If a caregiver has confidence that a patient can heal, the patient will synchronize with those feelings and start believing she can heal, too. The caregiver's intention drives the energy of the interaction, which can influence the patient's belief that she can get better. Seeing her as potentially healthy and well creates the positive expectancy in her that results in better health.

Breast cancer advocate Lillie Shockney provides an example of how a connected synchronicity can be strategically used toward a positive outcome. This two-time breast cancer survivor is an author, nurse, and administrative director of the Johns Hopkins Breast Center.

Imagine a woman has found a lump in her breast and is waiting to see the oncologist. She is frightened about the "what ifs" and the potential loss of control in her life—not to mention her breasts. Then a vibrant, strong, and confident nurse walks through the door and makes her feel as if she is the most important person in the world. The nurse says calmly and directly, "Hi, my name is Lillie Shockney. I've sat where you're sitting. I know what you're feeling. I'm going to help you get through this. I've had breast cancer twice. And I've had two mastectomies."[16]

Understanding that all of the explanatory pamphlets in the world won't assuage the anxiety a breast cancer diagnosis can evoke, Shockney opens her blouse to show this new patient her reconstructed breasts. "Feel that," she says, confident that her breasts are relatively natural. This type of plastic surgery relies on transplanted abdominal fatty tissue. "The bonus tummy tuck is a silver lining," Lillie adds with a laugh. She then touches the woman's knee and proclaims, "This is doable." Soon they are both talking about future treatments and laughing.

Why is Shockney so good at this interaction? She has insight into what the patient is experiencing. She makes her feel special and devotes her full attention. She shows the patient that they have something in common, and that she is not alone in this struggle. She uses appropriate humor to lighten the fear. And most importantly, Lillie gives the woman confidence that she can pull through this, too. That statement, "This is doable," is so important. In a matter of minutes, her art of interactive synchrony creates neuropeptides and hormones in the patient's brain that travel throughout her body, facilitating confidence. There is less fear and more optimism, and the immune system works stronger. Much like participating in a support group, having someone like Shockney on their team gives people hope and direction that they can get to a better place.

In order to motivate people to make healthful changes or support them through a difficult time, often the tipping point is this connection with someone who believes they can heal. And that connection can be found in shared brain circuits.

THE POSITIVE EFFECTS OF THE HORMONE OXYTOCIN

Hormones are chemical messengers secreted by the brain, reproductive organs, and elsewhere in the body that travel in the bloodstream to other organs where they exert an effect. In a graceful, reciprocal dance, hormones influence behavior, but behavior also influences the release of hormones. For example, if a person stands waving his arms and pumping his fists in the air as if he'd just won a race, his testosterone levels will rise.[17]

When it comes to making the connection, oxytocin is a wonder-hormone. Originally, it was understood to primarily be a muscle-contracting agent. Secreted during childbirth, it causes uterine contractions during labor and triggers milk ejection when women are breast feeding. (The drug Pitocin is a form of oxytocin that is administered to induce labor and speed along a lagging delivery.)

Because oxytocin is abundant in a new mother's bloodstream when she first gazes into the eyes of her infant, it is also thought to play an important role in mother-infant bonding. An early experiment with virgin female rats helped to prove this. These rats, which are not known for their motherliness (they're anxious around newborn pups and can ignore or even eat them), were injected with blood from a female that had just given birth. The otherwise hostile virgins suddenly behaved like nurturing mothers, licking the pups and protecting them. It is believed that oxytocin helped to alter the virgin rats' behaviors.[18]

Oxytocin has been found to enhance intimacy not just

between mother and child, but also among strangers, lowering the activity of the amygdala (the fear center in the brain) so that people can get to know one another—say at a party or bar—without stress.[19] With partners, it is secreted in both genders during sexual activity (albeit in higher levels among women), after orgasm, and when sleeping together. Dubbed "the love hormone," it increases a person's desire to be physically connected with others, and that connection is good for one's health and well-being. Hugging releases oxytocin, which also lowers blood pressure, regulates heart rate, and reduces stress hormones like cortisol—especially in women.[20] One recent investigation found that it helped men lose weight.[21] It's also thought to drive women's tendency to huddle with other women and children when danger is near (to "tend and befriend" as compared with the fight-or-flight impulse so prevalent in men).[22] Researchers have found that people with higher oxytocin levels are apt to be calmer, more empathic and sociable, and less anxious. In another graceful, reciprocal dance, everyone wants to be around individuals who exhibit these attributes. Perhaps that's because, by engaging others' mirror neurons, people with high oxytocin levels may trigger those positive feelings in them.

In addition to these really important social benefits, recent research has demonstrated that oxytocin can also have pain-relieving effects. In one study testing whether oxytocin enhances the healing (placebo) response, scientists in Germany sprayed either the hormone or saline solution (plain salt water) into the nostrils of eighty male volunteers. Then they applied two patches of ointment on these men's forearms. The volunteers were told that one cream had an anesthetic in it and the other did not. But, in fact, neither of these creams had any active ingredients; they were both inert. The next step was to wait fifteen minutes while the "anesthetic" cream took effect. During this time, a calibration procedure was performed on each person to identify the intensity at which a twenty-second painful heat stimulus was perceived as a 60 on a scale of 0 to 100. Then the heat stimulus was applied ten times to each spot on the arm. The researchers found that even though both ointments were inactive, the volunteers reported less pain in the area rubbed with the "painkiller" cream. This is in line with other studies that demonstrate the healing effect that I discussed earlier. But even more interesting, the people who had received the oxytocin nose spray felt almost 58 percent less pain than those who'd gotten the saline.[23] The oxytocin had greatly enhanced the pain-relieving effects of the inert creams. In essence, it rendered the pain less painful.

Bear in mind that oxytocin itself does not act like an opioid—any woman in labor can attest to that. Nevertheless, after I deliver a baby, the most effective pain reliever I can give a mother to keep her from feeling the repair of a vaginal tear is her new baby in her arms. The take-home message for me from this research is that since oxytocin is released when people connect, that alone reduces pain, suffering, stress, and anxiety. Indeed, hugs and hand-holding may actually work in ways that scientists are still exploring.

In one such study, Sheldon Cohen at Carnegie Mellon University found that the number of meaningful relationships a person has is inversely related to his or her susceptibility to the common cold.[24] In 2014, Dr. Cohen and his team took this one step further: they counted how many hugs and how much conflict their 404 research subjects experienced over a two-week period. They then exposed their subjects to a cold virus and monitored them in quarantine. Perhaps not surprisingly, the people who had higher levels of conflict and less support in their lives were more likely to become ill. However, among infected participants, those with greater support and more frequent hugs were protected against stress and had less severe colds.[25] Could this be true because oxytocin levels increase with touching and hugging? I would venture that it is. Yet, paradoxically, one would expect more colds with hugging due to close physical contact during which the virus could be spread.

Consider this: Oxytocin levels go up in sorority houses when women cycle their menses together. They go up in wolf packs when a pup is born. They go up when we hold hands and hug. The more connected we are, the more there is a rise in the "love hormone," the better we feel, and the stronger our immune defenses become.

NEUROPLASTICITY

As researchers have been able to peer into brains in action using fMRIs that track activity, they have learned that the adult brain is not static, as was once believed. Instead, it continues to grow and develop over a person's lifetime in a process called neuroplasticity. It's never too late to change or learn something new.

For instance, investigations of people who had been blind since birth have found that the occipital (visual) lobe, the part of the brain normally used for seeing, is now recruited by fingers feeling and interpreting Braille letters.[26] Research conducted by Edward Taub, a behavioral neuroscientist at the University of Alabama at Birmingham, evaluated people who suffered paralysis of one side of the body due to a stroke. He showed that when the functional arm was bound up and prevented from moving for several weeks, the "paralyzed" arm started to work. Essentially, engaging the process of neuroplasticity, the stroke patient's brain created workarounds to bypass the area that was injured, either by relying on adjacent areas to take over or a complete reorganization of function.[27] A number of other case studies have shown that when one part of the brain is removed to treat severe seizures, another area adapts to perform the functions of the missing neurons.[28]

The same concept is at work when ophthalmologists patch the good eye of a child with strabismus, a condition in which the eyes aim in different directions. Strabismus is the most common cause of amblyopia, also known as "lazy eye," which occurs when the brain ignores some or all of the input from one eye. Patching the more functional eye stimulates the brain to develop new neuro-networks in the occipital lobe, which help the lazy eye to "see." And other research has found that specialized parts of the brain grow bigger than "normal" when people engage in certain activities—for example, the motor cortex area dedicated to moving the left fingers is much larger in violin virtuosos than in people who don't play the instrument. This brain growth can even occur with mental activity alone. At Harvard University, for instance, research conducted by Alvaro Pascual-Leone found that the motor cortex of volunteers playing an easy five-finger piano piece increased after a week of intensive practicing, as expected. But perhaps surprisingly, the motor cortex of the control group also grew, even though their instructions were only to *imagine* that they were playing the piece. Simply thinking about the music changed these volunteers' brains.[29]

It's also true that neuroplasticity can play a negative role. For instance, the brain shrinks when someone is in chronic pain.[30] But when that person works with a therapist to explore his or her issues more deeply, the therapeutic connection is associated with the regrowth of brain tissue in the prefrontal cortex, the area associated with higher thought such as planning, decision making, and the expression of personality.[31]

These studies point to the brain's plasticity—its ability to re-create itself—depending on environment and stimulation. As my friend and colleague, neuroscientist Richard Davidson has so eloquently stated, "Nature has endowed the human brain with a malleability and flexibility that lets it adapt to the demands of the world it finds itself in. The brain is neither immutable nor static but continuously remodeled by the lives we lead.[32]

What does this mean for people who want to connect with others to help in their healing? When it comes to the connection, the simple brain plasticity principle is *If we use it, we build it*. Just like the person mastering the violin, the compassionate part of one's brain—the left frontal lobes—grows and develops with practice, as Richard Davidson showed in his research with Tibetan monks who practiced compassionate mindful meditations.[33] If individuals desire to become good at serving and healing others, they must reinforce these parts of their brain. They have to "practice the violin," so to speak.

As caregivers master the art of connecting, they create change in the neuroplasticity potential of their own brains. Once they do this, they can bring to bear their own sense of hope, empathy, and optimism to help their patients or loved ones develop and reinforce new and more healthful neural pathways.

This is why human connection is the remedy for burnout. A study at the Mayo Clinic found that 54.4 percent of physicians have at least one symptom of burnout.[34] This is related to trying to fit the complexity of a patient's life and health into a fifteen-minute office visit, during which most of the time is spent focusing on a computer and not a human being. Such a lack of connectedness can cause physical pain, just as it did for me when I interacted with the young girl whom we called patient number 406 in our study.

Caregivers have the power to positively influence neuroplastic potential in themselves and others, but in order to do this, they must modify their own brains through epigenetic influences.

THE ROLE OF EPIGENETICS

Similar to the changes to neurons in the brain due to neuroplasticity, our genes also listen and respond to the choices we make. Today, researchers are finding that genes do not necessarily dictate one's destiny, as was previously believed. Although people can't alter the genes they inherit, variations in their expression can be caused by external or environmental factors that switch them on or off to trigger or halt the production of specific proteins. The new scientific discipline that investigates how genes express themselves is called epigenetics. It is the study of what happens *around* one's genes.

Consider how this works with the honeybee. All the bees in a hive are genetically identical. But the hive chooses one bee to become the queen. They bathe this potential queen in royal jelly, which is high in nutrient value. She grows 20 percent larger than her fellow worker bees, and she lives 20 percent longer even though her DNA is no different from her former peers'.[35]

Many epigenetic studies have been conducted with rodents. For instance, in a side-by-side comparison of brain cells, the dendrites (the branching ends of the cells that communicate with other neurons) of rat pups that were consistently licked and groomed grew much more than those that had more neglectful mothers. It was shown that the pups with attentive mothers grew into adults with better cognitive functioning and enhanced learning in stressful environments.[36] In other experiments, rats that had been born of anxious, fearful, negligent mothers but raised by calm, attentive ones also became calm . . . and raised mellow pups themselves. The reverse was also true. Those born to nurturing mothers but raised by jumpy ones became skittish and gave birth to similar pups. This wasn't just learned behavior. Upon further examination, it was discovered that the mother's attentiveness or fearfulness caused genes that altered stress receptors in the pups' brains to be turned on or off.[37] Other well-known studies have shown that when researchers fed pregnant mice nutrient-rich diets, their offspring maintained a normal weight throughout their lifetimes, despite the mice being bred for a genetic predisposition for diabetes and obesity. We can nurture nature.

Now consider research conducted by well-known physician Dean Ornish on people. He studied how environment and diet affect heart disease and early prostate cancer in men. His findings regarding prostate cancer are impressive. Men with low-grade prostate cancer in an experimental group of forty-four volunteers followed a low-fat, plant-based diet; enjoyed sixty minutes of a stress reduction activity daily; exercised regularly; and continued to have strong social connections. These activities had a positive influence on the genes that coded for prostate cancer. The growth of cancer cells in the men who were part of the experimental group was inhibited almost eight times as much as those in the control group.[38] Essentially, the interventions that Dr. Ornish recommended turned off the genes for prostate cancer. After one year, none of the men in the experimental group needed conventional treatments compared with six of the forty-nine men in the control group. Prostate specific antigen (PSA), a blood marker for prostate cancer, decreased 4 percent in the experimental group as compared to a 6 percent *increase* in the control group. These results indicate that intensive lifestyle changes may affect the genetic progression of early, low-grade prostate cancer.

What does all of this mean for caregivers? We know that genes can be activated or deactivated by environment and lifestyle—whether people eat health-enhancing foods, whether they exercise sufficiently, whether they have experienced trauma, whether they forgive someone who has hurt them or carry around a big grudge. All of these factors can influence genes' production of healthy or diseased proteins. Some scientists have predicted that as much as 98 percent of the gene-related diseases that occur in the industrialized world are associated with factors that are outside the actual chromosomes. What surrounds the gene can turn it on or off.

98 Percent Epigenetic Influence

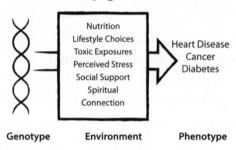

| Genotype | Environment | Phenotype |

How does epigenetics work? Take the gene called *RS993609*, which is a variant of *FTO*, a gene associated with fat mass and obesity. People with the *FTO* gene are more likely to become overweight while people without it are less likely. But in a study of Amish people who carried this gene,[39] most were slim. The fact that they averaged eighteen thousand steps a day (nearly nine miles) might have had something to do with it. In this case, genetic risk did not lead to an unfavorable outcome because environmental factors intervened.

Another group of researchers evaluated the weight variations in participants of the Framingham Heart Study, originally a database of 5,209 adults who lived in Framingham, Massachusetts, that was collected in 1948 to better understand the risks of heart disease. These researchers identified the original participants and their children and grandchildren who carried the *FTO* gene and noticed a significant increase in obesity rates after World War II. Environmental changes such as modern conveniences and tech advances (which have reduced the need for physical activity), coupled with increased caloric intake due to reliance on processed foods, have resulted in a significant increase in obesity.[40] It's not that more people have the *FTO* gene, but that gene is now being expressed more often because of lifestyle influences. *What people do influences the expression of their genes.*

How does this relate to the connection?

Our medical system focuses on a person being sick and broken. The current physicians' diagnostic code book, the *International Statistical Classification of Diseases and Related Health Problems* (ICD-10) lists more than 68,000 possible diagnoses. The previous iteration, the ICD-9, which is nearly 20 years old, had merely 13,000 codes. Are people getting sicker? Well, that depends on whom you ask. New medical conditions found in the updated code book include such disorders as "being struck by a duck" and "burn due to water skis catching on fire." The same is true for the psychologists' diagnostic manual, the DSM, which classifies psychiatric conditions. The first edition began with 106 entries. There are now more than 500 when you add subsets of psychiatric diagnosis from the latest edition. Is the increase in possible diagnoses really improving the treatment of mental illnesses? I think not. It is helping clinicians better catalog disease, attach treatments to specific conditions, and extract payments from medical insurance or other sources. But the concerning aspect of this labeling trend is worsening fragmentation of care.

How? If reimbursement is tied to what is wrong with patients, that becomes the principal focus. This coding system does not encourage the exploration of how people's lives are related to the diagnostic labels they are given. It may matter more to patients to have someone who cares and wants to help them than the drugs they take or the labels they are given. If they have a compassionate person in their lives, the drugs are likely to work better, and they will need to be labeled not as "recurring depression," but as "Betty with a unique story who once had depression." The process of connecting should drive the system, not the diagnostic labels given to broken parts. Imagine if we change the neuroplasticity of the health care system. What effect could that have on the epigenetic potential of human beings?

Besides, all of this attention to diagnosis focuses on the wrong aspect of health. We set intention by what we give attention to. These thousands of diagnoses highlight what's wrong with us. The health system is in need of a shift from just focusing on what's the matter with people, to what matters to people . . . and how we can use what is meaningful as motivation toward health.

Epigenetics teaches that one's intentions can influence physical reality. From my experience, how caregivers are with people—the environment they create around them—could impact the genetic expression of their genes. Once caregivers see another person as potentially healthy instead of broken, they redirect their own energy toward health. Belief in someone's self-healing potential is the first, most important step in stimulating their neuro-networks and chemicals to facilitate healing.

Once caregivers believe in this self-healing potential, others feel and believe it, too, just like the mirror neurons and the synergistic effects in the brains of those with whom we have a connection. This mind-set, in itself, creates an intention that can have an epigenetic influence on one's DNA that moves patients toward the healing process.

WIRED FOR COMPASSION

Social psychologist Dacher Keltner tells us that "Compassion is a biologically based emotion rooted deep in the mammalian brain, and shaped by perhaps the most potent of selection pressures humans evolved to adapt to—the need to care for the vulnerable."[41] This feeling is so strongly ingrained in our species, we see it from birth. We have all observed newborns crying in the hospital nursery in response to other wailing babies around them—a very early expression of mirror neurons and emotional contagion.

In fact, three- and six-month-old infants have been shown to react to compassion and turn away from negativity—long before their parents have socialized them to be kind, sharing, or helpful. In a series of ingenious studies, J. Kiley Hamlin at the University of British Columbia and her team tested eleven infants to observe their reactions to helping or hindering situations. As the babies sat in an infant seat or were held on a parent's lap, they looked at a stage with a white background and the image of a green hill that had a plateau about one-third of the way up. The babies watched a "climber"—a red circle with googly eyes—try to make it up the hill. It failed twice, partially sliding back down. During a third try, it was either pushed up the hill by a "helper" shape or bumped to the bottom by a "hinderer." The researchers measured how long the infants looked at the various characters and whether they reached out for them—well established signs of infants' preferences. They found that the babies preferred the character that helped the climber over the one that impeded its progress. All eleven infants ultimately reached for the helper, and ten of them looked longer at it.[42]

We are, indeed, wired to be caregivers. Neuroscience shows that people take pleasure in helping others. The brain's reward center (the nucleus accumbens, which is rich in dopamine receptors) is quite active when we are giving and cooperative.[43] But perhaps the most interesting neurological underpinning of compassion is the vagus nerve. Psychophysiologist Stephen Porges, currently "Distinguished University Scientist" at the Kinsey Institute at Indiana University Bloomington, found that this large system of nerves, a part of the autonomic nervous system, connects to a network of oxytocin receptors. It also helps slow the heart and breathing and controls some facial nerves and vocal apparatus—initiating the short, soothing sigh that people always emit when they're concerned about others' suffering.[44]

At the University of California, Berkeley, then-student Chris Oveis sought to prove the involvement of this nerve. As he showed a group of participants slides of people who were suffering undeservedly (starving children, for instance) to elicit compassion and a second group of slides that would evoke pride (landmarks at the university), he measured the activation of the vagus nerve. He found that feelings of compassion for the anguished increased the activity of this nerve.[45] Other researchers have now linked the vagus nerve to altruistic behaviors. As social psychologist Dacher Keltner explains, "It is an active concern for others, and not a simple mirroring of others' suffering, that is the fount of compassion, and that leads to altruistic ends."[46]

We humans are wired from birth to connect and to be of service to others. The vagus nerve travels through the diaphragm and is naturally stimulated with simple, deep breathing exercises as would occur during yoga or other meditations. Caregivers who are sitting with a person in a difficult situation can activate their own vagus nerve by breathing deeply (as if they're blowing up a balloon inside their bodies beneath their belly button) to release dopamine, stimulate the relaxation response, and improve immunity within themselves.

But the innate ability to connect erodes or is hidden if we have been hurt, abused, or deprived of love and support. Our inborn compassion is a seed that needs to be nourished and watered. If unsupported, its potential neither grows nor blooms. But the potential is always there, waiting for the right conditions to set it into motion.

. . .

Prompted by human biology, people can create the intention to move together toward a better place. Caring for others through connection is the most powerful tool. It results in the release of positive neurochemicals, brain growth, and genetic manipulation that can bring everyone closer to a more meaningful and healthier life. This is how people create an optimally healthy environment for those they care about and themselves.

We get what we give. And when we care for others, we get just as much out of it as they do. Just like the twelve-year-old patient number 406 in our cold study tried to reach out to me in a kind, compassionate way. She could see that I needed more help than she did, and she was the one with the cold in the doctor's office! We all have an innate ability to want to help others that sets in motion our own innate ability to heal ourselves.

4

Make Health Primary

Those who have a "why" to live can bear with almost any "how."

—VIKTOR E. FRANKL, *Man's Search for Meaning*[1]

A person's well-being is often linked to the big picture—his or her sense of meaning and purpose. I have often found that in our systems of care, caregivers attempt to "fix" problems superficially rather than taking the time to seek out and cure the core issues that may lie beneath them. But there is much to be learned from Jewish survivors of Nazi concentration camps about the significance of one's meaning and purpose for longevity and joie de vivre.

LESSONS FROM SURVIVORS OF NAZI CONCENTRATION CAMPS

The vital importance of a sense of meaning and purpose became clear a few decades ago to the American Israeli medical

sociologist Aaron Antonovsky, who was interested in understanding what he called the "origin of health." In his studies,
he investigated a population that had been through extreme
trauma: survivors of the Holocaust. In a group of Israeli women
over age fifty who had emigrated from Eastern Europe after
World War II, he found, as he expected, that those who had
survived concentration camps more than a quarter century
earlier tended to be less well-adjusted than women of the same
age who had not been camp inmates. The camp survivors had
greater emotional stress and more worries, and overall they
derived less pleasure from their activities than the other group
of women.[2]

But the big surprise of the study, Antonovsky wrote, was that
an impressive number of the camp survivors were doing quite
well. Twenty-five years after the end of the war, nearly 40 percent were in excellent physical health for women of their age.
Twenty-nine percent showed no sign of emotional symptoms or
"malfunctioning." Many were involved in a range of activities
and described themselves as happy. When it came to ranking
the satisfaction they got from their lives, nearly 30 percent rated
their daily experience at least an 8 out of a top score of 10.

Antonovsky felt this unexpected finding was worthy of discussion. "Where did their health come from?" he wondered.
"What has enabled some women, subjected to the most destructive experiences conceivable, to lead well-adapted lives?"
Antonovsky put the ultimate question this way: In the tumultu-
ous "stream of life . . . whose nature is determined by historical,
social-cultural, and physical environmental conditions—what
shapes one's ability to swim well?"

Antonovsky suggested a few answers. For one, he thought the women's traumatic experiences may have helped them devise strategies to put their everyday stresses into perspective. But perhaps most significantly, the women had developed meaningful roles in their new lives—as wives, mothers, friends, and professionals—and these helped define and sustain them. In writing about "swimming well," Antonovsky coined the term "*salutogenesis*" (from the Latin *salus*, meaning health, and the Greek, *genesis*, meaning origin) to describe the importance of a health-promoting worldview, one that encourages people to develop the appropriate skills and resilience to navigate life's tumult.

"HEALTHY" VERSUS "SICK"

Antonovsky's various theories about health have been used in the developing field of psychoneuroimmunology. But the term he developed, "salutogenesis," is particularly helpful overall. It describes how professional and family caregivers might think about serving people.

Most of the time, when someone is hurting, helpers focus on the state of illness—on "pathogenesis." (Doctors, especially, are trained to pursue what's wrong and provide direct solutions.) They attend to the cause of a disease and its treatment. For many conditions, like cancers that must be considered with great specificity, a pathogenic approach is essential. But Antonovsky believed that the most important ingredient for *health* was defining a personal sense of meaning. In other words, to sustain themselves, people must believe that their lives have a purpose. A salutogenic attitude toward health care, therefore, focuses less on the disease and more on the individual as *potentially healthy*. It looks for a person's sources of meaning—such as family, career, creativity, friendships, and spirituality—and uses them as both the route to better health and the ultimate goal.

I believe that this positive attitude is a powerful addition to the way caregivers can engage in serving people. Some medical disciplines have already begun exploring how individuals' sense of meaning impacts their health outcomes. For one thing, happiness is a relative concept. In one study, there was no significant difference in happiness among new paraplegics and lottery winners after a certain amount of time passed.[3] Several recent studies in rehabilitation medicine have shown how spirituality affects patients' recovery from traumatic brain injury. One investigation found that people who described themselves as having a strong personal devotion to a higher power had better outcomes than others—even better than those who participated regularly in religious activities.[4] In other words, the researchers could predict better outcomes for those who could draw on their sense of meaning than those who were simply going through the motions.

In fact, the salutogenic shift in focus takes into consideration that when people shine a spotlight on something, they can heighten its presence. If they want more health, they have to give it their attention. In this chapter, I focus on the power of the positive, the possible, and the potential to increase health and improve outcomes. However, first we need to understand the dark side of this equation.

THE TOLL OF THE NEGATIVE

Many studies in recent years have documented the way mind-centered problems like chronic stress can cause physiological damage to the body. Stress is now widely known to heighten harmful levels of the steroid cortisol, a change that can lead to heart disease, sleep disorders, and digestive problems. These effects can persist throughout life.

A study by Vincent Felitti and Robert Anda published in the *American Journal of Preventive Medicine* entitled "Relationship of Childhood Abuse and Household Dysfunction to Many of the Leading Causes of Death in Adults,"[5] made a very strong case for how emotional trauma in childhood can undermine physiological health for a lifetime. Dr. Felitti had been a weight loss specialist at a Kaiser Permanente hospital in Southern California. In that capacity, he had helped one of his obese patients lose more than one hundred pounds of excess weight—a great triumph for both of them.

But after only a few months, his patient regained all that weight and more. Rather than throw his hands up in frustration, however, Dr. Felitti had an open and frank conversation with this young woman. He made the connection. Their discussion revealed that his patient had been the victim of childhood sexual abuse at the hands of her grandfather—a situation for which she felt great shame and pain. But now, her newly improved figure had attracted the attention of an older male coworker. Rather than making her happy, his flirtatiousness sent her into a tailspin. Fearing sexual contact, she once again consoled herself with food, padding her body with excess weight as a defense while risking the plethora of destructive health issues that accompany obesity.

Upset but also fascinated by this woman's situation, Dr. Felitti began interviewing all of his obese patients. Soon he and his colleagues set upon a much more ambitious project. After having analyzed the medical records of eighteen thousand patients at the hospital, they made a surprising discovery. As Dr. Felitti put it, "Time does not heal some of the adverse experiences of childhood. We came to recognize that the earliest years of infancy and childhood are not lost, but like a child's footprints in wet cement, are often lifelong."[6] These "adverse childhood experiences" (which he called ACE) are all *emotional*. They include categories of abuse (psychological, by parents; physical, by parents; sexual, by anyone), emotional or physical neglect, poverty, housing instability, discrimination, family conflict, and household dysfunction (alcoholism or drug use in homes, loss of biological parents before the age of eighteen, depression or mental illness in the home, mother treated violently, and/ or imprisoned household member). These emotional traumas were strongly correlated with *physiological* adult disorders such as cardiovascular disease, cancer, chronic lung disease, bone fractures, and liver disease as well as psychological issues such as hopelessness, anxiety, and divorce. In fact, 61.4 percent of the people in this study had a mental health condition that disturbed their work or other activities for two weeks or more.

Protective factors would include safe, cohesive neighborhoods; parental warmth and involvement; a connection with a caring adult (counselor, clergy, relative); and a parent who did not suffer trauma.

Another example of how a negative mind-set can harm health outcomes occurs when caregivers take a pathogenic approach and focus only on an illness and its symptoms. This attitude may even sustain a disease. For some people, paying incessant attention to their condition shapes their identity and becomes a comfort. Take, for example, this story relayed to me by a gastroenterologist who treated a woman with Crohn's disease. Over the years, Candace had taken great care of herself and had not only learned all she could about the disorder but had also become involved in Crohn's disease advocacy and fund-raising. She had even become the leader of a local support group.

At a certain point, following some tests, the gastroenterologist told Candace during an office visit that he had good news: she likely did not have Crohn's disease after all and could begin managing her condition with a different approach. He could not have been more astonished at her response. Candace stood up—and stormed out of his office. It became clear to her physician then that her focus on the ailment had helped shape how Candace saw herself. Recasting her symptoms in a new framework actually threw her sense of self and her identity into turmoil.

A constant focus on pathology can have such harmful effects. Some people who have chronic conditions come to view themselves as sick, above all other aspects of their being, and the rest of their lives become essentially paralyzed. Their ongoing medical needs—and even their interactions with physicians—can reinforce this self-image. In one study of women with fibromyalgia, many patients said their condition isolated them from doctors (who sometimes questioned the validity of their illness) and from friends (who were frustrated about suddenly canceled plans). Many complained that the disease had robbed them of their identity: "They no longer recognized the person that they once were and struggled to recognize the person that they had become." The pathology had eclipsed all other aspects of their lives.[7]

When people lose their previous sense of self, as in the case of these individuals, the disease becomes their new identity. It is then difficult for them to appreciate their lives outside of their ailment. In support groups for patients with fibromyalgia, these interactions can result in improvement or not. People in the groups who do not improve often engage in conversation about the severity of their complaints. This can create a sense of competition, each person vying to top the other when the symptom is the focus. On the other hand, research has shown that participants in support groups focusing on *stressful triggers* that may be at the root of their hypersensitive muscles showed significant improvement in pain. Sessions focused on structured, written, emotional disclosure and emotional awareness exercises. This had a larger pain reduction benefit than many of the medicines usually prescribed for this condition including gabapentin (Neurontin) and pregabalin (Lyrica). In fact, this intervention improved pain, tenderness, and self-reported physical function for at least six months compared with those in a control group who did not participate in the meetings.[8]

A HEALING PARADIGM

Pathogenesis focuses on the severity of pain and the difficulties that one encounters, but I am suggesting that we change the conversation to one that's hopeful and empowering. Opportunities for healing reside in moving from what's wrong with individuals' bodies toward what's important to them and gives their lives meaning. Most people need help in doing this—it's so much easier to accomplish when someone walks with them, providing support and encouragement. Caregivers are essential in this process. They can focus on patients' health goals by asking simple questions such as "What gives you energy to get up in the morning and go about your day?" This allows patients to see their lives with meaning despite their pain or disability. Other great questions: "If you weren't in pain, what would your life look like?" and "What do you want your health for?" A compassionate connection allows caregivers to help patients exchange their problem lists for their health lists—that is, to emphasize what they feel they need most to be healthy and resilient. This salutogenic approach helps caregivers focus on the person beyond the illness. In addition, it incorporates the idea that both mind and body can be engaged in the pursuit of health.

What individuals think and expect can change the course of their body's responses. Many studies have affirmed the physiological effects of positive expectations. As we've seen, placebos can play an important role in improving health and pain relief. Moreover, very recently, researchers in Virginia have found that the lymphatic system flows through the thinking and emotional parts of the brain (the anterior cingulate, orbitofrontal and insular cortices, the nucleus accumbens, amygdala, and peri-aqueductal gray matter) described in Chapter 2. Lymph carries immune cells. Prior to this, it was believed that it could not cross the blood/brain barrier and enter the brain. But now scientists know that there is a direct connection between emotions (as generated in the brain) and immune function. How people feel can affect their ability to fight diseases.[9]

Positive interactions and outlook can go a long way. In 1987 the *British Medical Journal* published a study from the University of Southampton in England that looked at whether patients with vague viral symptoms fared better when doctors used positive phrases in talking about the diagnosis and treatment. Researchers found people who were exposed to positive expectations such as "You likely have a rhinovirus that will cause you to have symptoms for 8 to 10 days," recovered from their symptoms faster. In contrast, when the physician offered more uncertain comments, such as "I am not sure what is wrong with you," or "I am not sure that the treatment I am going to give you will have an effect," patients' viral illnesses dragged on longer. Two weeks after the visit, the group of patients who had received positive comments had a 64 percent recovery rate, while the group that left with uncertain feedback had a recovery rate of only 39 percent.[10]

Why did some patients recover sooner? We could say that they benefited from the healing effect—their hopefulness and sense of control were heightened by their physician's positive attitude and expectations. Caregivers can bring positivity to bear as a healing tool when they encourage others to focus on what's functional, important, and worthwhile about their lives.

With ever-rising evidence about the various ways the mind and body interact in wellness and disease, clinicians might do well to think about care that is just as much salutogenic as it is pathogenic and that concertedly engages the power of the mind. This shift would use a person's own capacity for positive expectations and optimism, self-awareness, faith, self-motivation, and connectedness, all in the pursuit of "health."

A salutogenic perspective can restore confidence to address problems that seem insurmountable. It can help people understand their health in ways that don't diminish them (as some feel blamed for their weight or their lifestyle habits), but instead honor their strengths and their potential for self-healing.

THE POWER OF POSITIVE EXPECTATIONS

Much has been written over the years about self-fulfilling prophecies and how expectations shape outcomes. A lot of this research is based on the breakthrough work of Robert Rosenthal, then a professor of social psychology at Harvard University. In 1965 he conducted what has become the famous Oak School study in South San Francisco. Dr. Rosenthal wanted to see whether teachers' expectations influenced the IQs of their students, who in this case were minorities—their parents had come from Mexico, and Spanish was spoken in the home.[11]

Dr. Rosenthal and the principal of the school (a fellow-researcher in this study) tested the IQs of incoming first graders in traditional ways. Without divulging any of this information to their teachers or parents, they randomly assigned these first graders to two groups. They told the teachers of the first group that their kids were "average." They based this false assessment on the "Harvard Test of Inflected Acquisition"—a nonexistent intelligence test. The teachers of the second group, however, were informed that their students showed a "spurt" in intellectual growth and were more gifted—also based on this bogus test. In truth, the kids were placed in these groups arbitrarily and without regard to any test results.

After one year, Dr. Rosenthal retested the children's IQs. The outcome was astonishing. In the "average" group, the children's IQ increased by 12 points. In the so-called gifted group, however, IQ increases were more than double that of the "average" kids—27.4 points. The only reason for these differences was how the teachers treated the youngsters based on the former's expectations for performance. Dr. Rosenthal called these self-fulfilling prophecies the "Pygmalion effect in the classroom." In Greek mythology, Pygmalion was a sculptor who fell in love with his creation, and it came to life. As Dr. Rosenthal defined it, higher teacher expectations lead to improved student performance. The children whom they believed in came to life, just like Pygmalion's statue.

In 1978, Dr. Rosenthal conducted a meta-analysis that combined the results of 345 studies.[12] Again, he found that the positive effect of teachers' expectations on their students was very much like what other scientists have discovered about the placebo effect—a 30 percent improvement. His work clearly shows the power of positive expectations.

The same can be said of how people limit themselves by their perception of what's possible. In 1890 the U.S. Census Bureau first used the Hollerith tabulating machine (a punch card device that was an early precursor to IBM) to count the country's population. Workers were told that once they learned the rather complicated system, they were expected to process 550 cards a day. Those who went beyond this number felt stressed and anxious. However, a second group of 200 workers was hired and trained but not given any sense of how many cards they were expected to handle. Those employees processed 2,100 cards a day without any anxiety or stress.[13]

The world of sports is rife with these kinds of examples. For instance, it was thought impossible to run a mile in less than four minutes—so no one tried. Then, in 1954, Roger Bannister broke the "four-minute barrier" by 0.6 second, and now completing a mile in under four minutes has become standard for male middle-distance runners. If you don't believe in yourself or others, your lack of confidence becomes destiny. However, consider this: if you feel you're too small or insignificant to make a difference, try sleeping with a mosquito!

These are all illustrations of how the mind limits or frees and contributes to self-healing. Caregivers can easily translate these concepts to how they behave toward the people they want to serve. In health care, clinicians are usually too quick to say, "You need medication." Drugs suppress symptoms, true, but they also don't give the body the opportunity to heal itself. When the mind harbors the expectation that one will need to be on a certain drug forever, that becomes the physical reality. But if I, as a physician, give my patient hope and encourage him to believe in his unlimited potential for health, his body will do all it can to heal itself.

Faith that others can heal is a powerful piece of the connection. One of the most important things that I can do as a physician is believe that my patients can get to a better place. This drives our energy toward collectively finding a way.

However, it is injurious to overstress the importance of self-healing at the expense of a patient's well-being. For instance, if I am excessively optimistic and feel that the body can overcome any illness, I may push my patients too hard. Then, instead of helping, my adherence to a philosophical framework that is at variance with patients' true needs can cause a flare-up of the disease. I see this all the time in the management of chronic fatigue syndrome. One of the best treatments to stimulate energy production is the gradual titration of movement and exercise. But if doctors push their patients too quickly with overconfidence in the body's self-healing potential, they can trigger a relapse that results in worsening symptoms. We can cause harm if we don't appreciate the self-healing potential of the body, but we can also cause harm if we believe in it too much. Balance is an all-important component to healing.

HOW LARGE A ROLE CAN THE MIND ACTUALLY PLAY?

In our clinic, we saw a dramatic change in a particularly challenging patient when we took a salutogenic instead of a pathogenic approach with Maryann, a forty-year-old woman who had been plagued with myriad frustrating and hard-to-define symptoms. She was deeply fatigued, achy in her joints, generally run down, and seemed to be allergic to everything around her. She had headaches and intermittent nausea. She felt ter-

rible indoors and only mildly better outside. After testing negative for a wide range of conditions, she was beginning to feel
despair, having no way to understand what was happening to
her body or why she felt so wretched. On some level, she thought
that she was "going crazy." One diagnosis that had been suggested to her was multiple-chemical sensitivity (MCS), a condition that's poorly understood and that some in the medical
profession have disputed as being a real, organic disease caused
by external irritants. People with MCS feel they have become
intolerant of, or overly sensitive to, even low levels of chemicals.
Their symptoms vary from person to person, but the effects can
be wholly disabling, and there are no drugs or other therapies
to treat the condition.

But misgivings notwithstanding, having the label was one
step in the right direction for Maryann. It legitimized that her
body was going through something devastating and that her
suffering was real. She wasn't sure, however, how she felt about
it. Adam Rindfliesch, the practitioner in our clinic who was
seeing Maryann, invited her to consider her diagnosis from
a different angle. Instead of perceiving herself as a victim of
chemicals or irritants in her environment, in other words, constantly oppressed by her surroundings, she could appreciate her
physical response as a manifestation of her personal strengths.
She was reacting to chemicals because she was quite attuned to
her environment. Her sensitivity to their presence was a special
awareness she possessed. Many people with this condition are
highly intuitive. So instead of viewing her condition as a defect
in her body's immune system, she was encouraged to reframe
her response and understand it as part of the gift of being a

highly sensitive individual. This interpretation fit how she saw herself, in fact, as an artist and a sensitive soul.

The conversation represented an important turning point for Maryann. She had a diagnosis, which helped affirm her physical distress. Over time, she developed a keener understanding about when her symptoms would occur and found that she was better able to anticipate and tolerate the effects on her body. But she also began to comprehend her physical symptoms differently, as part of her unique personality and her approach to the world. When she and her physician made a plan for her treatment, she felt good about the idea of getting at the root of how she saw herself and coaxing her body into a more balanced state. As a highly sensitive individual, Maryann was often anxious and had what we call elevated "sympathetic tone"—that is, her fight-or-flight response was always on overdrive. So she was encouraged to mediate her tension with deep breathing exercises, meditation, and physical activity. Stimulants such as caffeine were eliminated from her diet.

If all we can do in health care is reduce fear (for patients as well as providers), we will have eliminated many downstream effects. This was true in Maryann's case. Her anxiety abated and she became less depressed and self-critical. She was still quite sensitive, of course, but her reaction to chemicals was reduced by 70 percent. The interactions between Maryann and her doctors involved an awareness that the words expressed during the appointment shaped how she faced her condition. In redefining how she perceived her situation, the conversation engaged her hopefulness, her self-esteem, and her ability to help herself.

Ultimately, her new outlook enabled her to improve the quality of her life.

As research reveals more about how the mind and body are interconnected, the salutogenic approach could be an important addition to the training of health professionals and family caregivers. Recently I visited a campus to give a lecture to a group of health providers about the importance of interpersonal connections in treating patients and promoting health. The funny thing is, people often respond as if the healing power of interpersonal connections is a new idea. Or, perhaps more poignantly, they respond as if they'd once known it but had somehow forgotten.

In a lecture hall filled with students, I posed this question: "If you were going to assemble a health team to address a patient's kidney failure, who would you recruit?" Hands shot into the air, and the students began suggesting a team of crackerjack specialists. "A nephrologist," one student said. "A surgeon," added another. "A dialysis nurse," another person called out. "A dialysis machine technician," said one more. "A pharmacist." Soon we had assembled a list of specialists who could navigate through a kidney crisis, and in fact, the necessary team to keep an ailing patient alive.

Then I asked them: "If you were going to assemble a team to keep an individual *healthy*, who would you recruit?" The beginning of the list contained a few of the usual suspects: a primary care doctor, a nurse . . . But then the list began to evolve. "A psychologist," one person said, "to help people deal with stress." As they thought more about the steps involved in staying healthy, students added a nutritionist to the team, and a social worker, and a personal trainer. One student said, "A chaplain, or some-one who could be a spiritual guide."

Then a student added, "A clown." A hesitant giggle rolled through the room as the student explained, "People feel better when they laugh."

Suddenly the list grew in ways that took the students by surprise.

"A grandmother," one said.

"A pet," another added.

As the students began to build the "team," taking into consideration all of the components that feel like health, a fundamental truth became clear: highly technical medical care is important when we need to deal with illness, but our well-being requires much more.

Health unites and disease segregates. Often people believe they need to be an expert or have a specialized degree to treat disease, but everyone can talk about health. Exploring it brings people together because they all have intuition as to what people need to become well. Often it is the children, the ones with the beginner's mind, who see it most clearly. It is also important to realize that caregivers can't become experts in salutogenesis without exploring and recruiting the nonphysical (spiritual, emotional, and meaningful) parts of others' lives. *But caregivers often treat just the physical aspects of disease because they live in the illusion that they can offer only physical cures.*

To be truly healthy, people need care from those who can address and engage what's at the core of their being. And to provide that care for others, to be "experts" in health and healing, caregivers will do better when they draw from skills beyond their book knowledge. Just like a child who knows how to offer a hug at exactly the right moment, they have the ability to draw from their own humanness. When they put those talents to use in a concerted and practiced way, they bring a much more powerful approach to health and self-healing.

Through the compassionate connection, caregivers are able to pull health from within. If they can encourage those whom they serve to find meaning and purpose and to connect to what they love, the body does all it can to heal.

5

Good Intentions Gone Bad

Some you win, my lady, and some you learn.
—From *The Second Best Exotic Marigold Hotel*

During my first year out of residency, in my primary care practice in Idaho, I treated a patient named Carl—an army veteran and ex-smoker with severe emphysema. He was prone to recurring bouts of pneumonia and had required increasing amounts of oxygen because his respiratory function was gradually diminishing. During his visit that day, he didn't have a severe infection. We were merely adjusting his inhaler medications. But I could see his prognosis playing out in a negative way over time. I was scared that my tools were no longer working for him. I believed that his condition was deteriorating and that his life expectancy was only six to twelve months. Because I was just out of residency (and quite green), I felt I needed to be open and honest with Carl and tell him that I felt that he should get his things in order as I did not foresee him living beyond another year.

This difficult task was challenging for me. I knew that I needed to convey to my patient the authentic reality of his condition. There is a way to do this that fosters hope and positive expectations. Unfortunately, I hadn't yet mastered those skills. So I explained to Carl, in what I felt was a kind and trusting way, that he should get his affairs in order. Given how his course was going, I thought he should have this information so he would have adequate time to prepare for the end. I did what I believed a good doctor should do, and he trusted me.

The next morning, I received a tearful call from his wife. "Carl died in his sleep last night," she said. I was stunned. Although this might well have been a sad coincidence, to this day, I wonder if my words had hastened his demise. *If I'd presented the information differently or not at all, would he still be alive? Did I create the expectation that he didn't have much longer to live?* I regret that I will never have the answers to these questions.

Of course, clinicians have to be strategic. If they know a patient is a rebel and a fighter, they might consider telling him that he doesn't have long to live. Some people benefit from such a statement. It mobilizes them, as they try to prove their doctors wrong. But others can collapse under the weight of this knowledge. As I have learned, everybody is different. Caregivers must know each patient's story and develop insight into their uniqueness so that they can use the best approach to help drive energy toward health. Otherwise, they can do more harm than good.

THE POTENTIAL FOR HARM

Humans are extraordinary creatures, capable of tremendous compassion. When others are having a hard time, they want to *help*. And they do help and even heal in many conscious and unconscious ways. But anything that has the capacity to create a positive effect can also create a harmful one. I see this in medicine all the time . . . the most powerful drugs for good have the most egregious side effects. The strongest antibiotics may cure nasty infections but they can also disrupt the flora in the gut. Antidepressants can lift a dark mood, but they can also cause sexual dysfunction and weight gain. Chemotherapy kills cancer cells but may poison the body in the process.

Our biological tools for connection—mirror neurons, oxytocin, brain plasticity, epigenetic influences, and hardwiring—can also, in a sense, betray caregivers and the people they serve. If clinicians are angry, despondent, or put-upon, patients will sense these emotions as well and may suffer as a result. Richard Davidson has said, "Feeling distress interferes with the desire to help, because if you're in pain yourself, you have little reserve for others' pain."[1] The fact is, sometimes what people say and do in moments when others are hurting unleashes more harm than was ever intended. And when caregivers mismanage those moments, they not only do a terrible disservice to those they care about and care for but they can also wreak long-term damage to relationships.

If caregivers have a good, trusting bond with someone, what they say may be injurious because the person who is hurting is more likely to be open to them and so absorb their statements and believe them more readily. In the very worst circumstances, people can be flippant, or joking, or insensitive at exactly the wrong moment. They may not mean to be cruel, but they respond to the other person's physical or emotional distress from *their own* insecurity, frustration, and fear, without considering the impact of the comment. This kind of help can be very damaging. It may drive wedges between friends and even isolate partners from each other in an affectionate, collaborative marriage. However, all is not lost in these instances. Nonverbal communication always supersedes the spoken word (see Chapter 8). If, through her behavior, a patient understands that his helper cares, he will forgive verbal transgressions because he knows her heart is true.

For those of us who wear the white coat, the stakes may be even higher. Physicians are perceived as authoritative figures, so patients are more likely to trust and believe them than people who aren't physicians. But that belief can also cause harm. Doctors have been called "explainaholics." According to James A. Tulsky, a developer of "Oncotalk," an instructional program for doctors treating cancer patients, "Our answer to distress is more information, that if a patient just understood it better, they would come around."[2] But answering a feeling with a fact never works for physicians (or, for that matter, family caregivers) since it does little to address the patient's underlying anxiety. When people who are suffering hear an unhelpful or callous comment from a doctor, especially at the most vulnerable moment of receiving a difficult diagnosis, they may hold on to that negative statement—and the anger they feel as a result—throughout their entire treatment and beyond.

WHEN PLACEBOS GO SOUTH:
THE NOCEBO EFFECT

When you stimulate the "healing effect" through a human interaction, the self-healing mechanisms of the body are set into motion through a dynamic flow of positive expectancy. This is orchestrated within the unique context of a person's life, cultivating hope and confidence toward getting to a better place. If both the caregiver and the person being helped truly believe this can be achieved, it often will be.

Along with the healing effect, however, there's also an equal and opposite phenomenon called the *nocebo effect*. In Latin, nocebo means "I shall harm." It works in much the same way as the healing effect, except in reverse—that is, negative beliefs can have damaging—sometimes even fatal—consequences, as I conjectured might have occurred with my patient Carl. A friend told me a gentle, nonmedical story of how this unfolded during her childhood. When she was learning to ride a two-wheeler, her father ran behind her as many parents did in those pre-training-wheel days, holding the back of the seat—or so she thought—to help her find her balance. In fact, with the positive belief that her father was supporting her, she rode quite a distance on her own. But when he didn't respond to a question she'd asked, and she turned around to see why, she realized that she had left him at least a block behind her. She had ridden all that way on her own while holding on to the *positive belief* that she was "safe." But as soon as she recognized that she was on her own, her *negative belief* that she didn't know how to ride a bike took over, and down she went.

The same issues occur in medicine with the deactivation of the healing effect. The mind not only can make people feel sicker but can actually produce harmful symptoms. In a study of forty people with asthma, for instance, participants were told they were going to be exposed to an irritant that could worsen their breathing. They were also informed that they would subsequently be given a new drug to treat their illness. However, the "irritant" sprayed into the air was only nebulized saline—simply aerated salt water. Immediately, 47.5 percent of patients developed airway restrictions, and 30 percent experienced a full-blown asthma attack. Just as significantly, when the patients in the study were given the "new asthma drug," every single one responded to the treatment—even though this remedy was also an inhalant consisting of the same aerosolized salt water.[3]

In another quite striking investigation,[4] a group of patients with Parkinson's disease underwent an experimental procedure in which a small hole was drilled into their skulls and cells from fetal brain tissue—as a replacement for the damaged area in their brains—were inserted in the spot believed to cause the disease. However, in this experiment (which probably would not be approved today because of stricter rules for studies in humans), the scientists also drilled holes in the skulls of a control group without inserting fetal cells.

As a whole, the experimental protocol did not work. There was evidence of brain growth among patients who received the fetal cells but no improvement in symptoms. In fact, those receiving the fetal cells developed worse dyskinesia (abnormal movements). But surprisingly, some of the people in the control group showed tremendous improvement of their Parkinson's symptoms. However, when these patients were informed at the end of the study that they did not receive the intervention, they became angry and frustrated. Once the truth sank in that no fetal cells were inserted, their symptoms recurred. That's the nocebo effect.

Why the people in the control group got better (placebo) and then worse (nocebo) may be related to fluctuations in dopamine levels. This reward hormone becomes deficient in Parkinson's disease, and as we learned in previous chapters, positive expectations influence its production, so it is an important player in the placebo effect as well. Dopamine increases with the administration of placebos and decreases with nocebos. Drilling a hole in the brain with the patient hoping and expecting to find benefit from this aggressive therapy may have worked by encouraging the brain to boost the production of dopamine—which would improve the patients' Parkinson's symptoms. But when they learned that they were in the control group, this realization made them feel tricked (nocebo), their dopamine levels declined, and their symptoms returned. It's just like learning to ride that bike: when my friend thought her dad was behind her, her dopamine levels were high, but when she realized that she was all alone, her dopamine levels dropped, and she fell.

Perhaps the most extreme examples of the nocebo effect are those of voodoo deaths. Many case studies describe how people who are perceived as having powers that some might portray as "black magic" have caused their targets to die if the latter had internalized a belief and an expectancy in the voodoo's potency.

Walter B. Cannon of Harvard Medical School conducted research into this phenomenon that is foundational to our current thinking about how the body's physiological responses can link emotions like fear with illness. In 1942, Dr. Cannon collected and published a series of anecdotes regarding voodoo death that were taken from Western medical observers of indigenous peoples in South America, Africa, Australia, New Zealand, the Pacific Islands, and Haiti.[5] The following is a particularly interesting description that Cannon reported as observed and recorded by Dr. Herbert Basedow in his 1925 book *The Australian Aboriginal.*

The man who discovers that he is being boned [that is, a bone is being pointed at him so that he is cursed] by any enemy is, indeed, a pitiable sight. He stands aghast, with his eyes staring at the treacherous pointer, and with his hands lifted as though to ward off the lethal medium, which he imagines is pouring into his body. His cheeks blanch and his eyes become glassy and the expression of his face becomes horribly distorted. . . . He attempts to shriek but usually the sound chokes in his throat, and all that one might see is froth at his mouth. His body begins to tremble and the muscles twist involuntarily. He sways backwards and falls to the ground, and after a short time appears to be in a swoon; but soon after he writhes as if in mortal agony, and, covering his face with his hands, begins to moan. After a while he becomes very composed and crawls to his wurley [a shelter made of branches and leaves]. From this time onwards he sickens and frets, refusing to eat and keeping aloof from the daily affairs of the tribe. Unless help is forthcoming in the shape of a counter-charm administered by the hands of the Nangarri, or medicine-man, his death is only a matter of a comparatively short time. If the coming of the medicine-man is opportune he might be saved.[6]

Once the medicine man or shaman removes the curse, the victim, previously so close to death, no longer has anything to fear. Dr. Basedow describes how he suddenly lifts his head, sits up, and asks for water, ready to rejoin the living.

Although Dr. Cannon and his predecessors lacked the EEGs and fMRIs we possess today to assess what was happening in the brains of people who felt cursed, nor did they have access to the analysis of the hormones, neurotransmitters, and neuropeptides involved in initiating these kinds of responses, still their observations that these individuals were quite literally frightened to death are valid. Today we can track the sequence of events that lead to such an outcome. Initially, the intended victims believed in the powers of the "witch doctor" or the enemy who was cursing them, and they became terrified. Their fear set off such a strong reaction, it caused a severe stimulation of the fight-or-flight process that is controlled by the sympathetic nervous system. That, in turn, triggered constriction of the blood vessels that reduced the blood supply to vital organs including the heart. With the ensuing cardiac arrhythmia and vascular collapse, the heartbeat became so weak, the believers died.[7]

Such brutal examples are more or less out of everyday experiences for most Westerners, but it can help explain how a less dramatic situation may also cause harm. For instance, women enrolled in the Framingham database with similar risk factors for cardiovascular disease were four times more likely to die if they *believed* they were predisposed to heart attacks as compared with those who did not harbor this belief.[8] This is not terribly different from reactions to a voodoo curse.

In another study published in the prestigious *New England Journal of Medicine,* researchers documented how some apparent heart attacks were reversible because they were caused by a spasm in a coronary artery. Actually, these are cases in which the heart is "stunned" due to sudden, severe emotional stress. The patients in this study who were diagnosed with "broken heart syndrome" suffered the symptoms and elevated cardiac enzymes of a heart attack, but the good news here is that they recovered completely.[9] This phenomenon is also named *tako-tsubo* cardiomyopathy, after a Japanese octopus trap. When the heart contracts normally, it generally transforms from the shape of a melon to that of a narrow potato. But with tako-tsubo, the heart is being choked. It actually resembles the narrow top of the trap that keeps an octopus from escaping once it has entered.

This disorder can be dangerous. A 2015 study that looked at a larger number of these takotsubo cardiomyopathy cases showed that individuals with the syndrome had a higher rate of death and some actually died from the event.[10] However, most of the heart attacks in the initial study were not treated in the traditional sense; the injury resolved on its own when the powerful emotion passed. When these patients underwent cardiac catheterizations to look for blockages of the coronary arteries, 90 percent of the angiograms were completely normal. Still, caregivers can learn a powerful lesson from this research: if a severe emotion can cause a reversible "heart attack," think of how positive feelings could help.

How to explain these "heart attacks"? The experience of Buddhist monks can be instructive. When their brain waves were tracked with an EEG while they were deep in a loving-kindness meditation (which I will explain in more detail in Chapter 10), they hardly responded to sudden, loud sounds such as gunshots. They didn't move; they didn't jump.[11] The sensors tracking their brain waves barely registered the blast. Upon hearing such an unexpected burst of deafening noise, most others would have startled or recoiled. We can trace these reactions back to the autonomic nervous system, which controls both action and rest. One element, the sympathetic nervous system, governs the fight-or-flight response while the other, the parasympathetic system, helps people relax. When these two systems become unbalanced, say tipping toward an apprehensive response, disease can occur. The more people live in a heightened state of anxiety, the more likely they are to be jarred, scream, or shout when an unexpected event disrupts their sense of peace. For instance, one of my friends—a high school administrator who worked with volatile teenagers involved in gangs—was wound up so tight, he would jump three inches off his chair when one of his sons dropped a fork during dinner. His sympathetic nervous system was set on overdrive.

Dr. Luana Colloca's study at the University of Turin that I mentioned in Chapter 1 in which postop patients received a powerful analgesic drug either directly from a clinician on their medical team or unannounced from an automatic infusion machine's IV drip, had an additional component. When a nurse came into the hospital rooms, turned off the drip, and announced to the patients, "We're stopping your pain medicine now," the patients experienced more pain than if the infusion machine's computer had turned off the IV automatically and without notice. How is this possible? With her actions, the patients felt that their trusted caregiver had betrayed them. This perception of betrayal caused suffering and harm.

WHAT DOESN'T HELP

I often tell the story of Carl's sudden and unexpected death to the medical students I teach in a course called The Healer's Art—one of my favorites, pioneered by Rachel Naomi Remen at the University of California, San Francisco. It's a five-session elective we offer to our first- and second-year students, as do ninety other medical schools across the country. Students write their own Hippocratic oath and examine why they want to do this work despite the many sacrifices and challenges it entails.

During the class, in an attempt to have our young doctor-trainees understand their patients and communicate with them more compassionately, we ask them to remember a time in their own lives when they'd experienced personal suffering such as the death of a loved one or the loss of something meaningful. Then we ask them to remember what someone did or said that was unhelpful or actually made them feel worse. Interestingly, in the fourteen years that we have been teaching this course, the answers have always been consistent between what helped and what didn't, suggesting that this is a universal human truth.

Here's what didn't work during a time of suffering:

- The person tried to explain it.
- The person told me, "Everything will all be okay."
- The person avoided me or changed the subject.
- The person tried to fix it.
- The person talked about her own experience.
- The person belittled my feelings.
- The person didn't allow me to cry or be sad.
- The person analyzed the situation.
- The person pushed his own spiritual beliefs.

Those words and actions ended up in the "did not help" column because people are often too quick to project their beliefs onto others without taking the time to listen and just be with them. Healing happens more as a result of one's presence and not so much from the advice that comes out of one's mouth. In order to do this well, caregivers need to pause, get out of their heads, and feel what the other person needs. (I provide ways to do this in Part II.) Turning away, placating, or changing the subject announces one's absence quite loudly. Analysis, judgment, criticism, and belittlement make people feel worse. Giving suggestions? Friends and family don't need knowledge; they need unconditional caring. There will be a time to advise them . . . maybe . . . but only if they ask.

This is really important when people are suffering. If they come to clinicians asking for advice on how to best manage diabetes, then it is appropriate to share cognitive knowledge. But if they've just lost a parent to a heart attack, they crave our hearts—literally. Remember the power of oxytocin? They need a kind presence and perhaps a hug, if they want one. They don't want us to "fix" the problem for them, because actually, we can't. Instead, we can help them move through the painful situation in a healthy way.

FIXING AND OTHER EXAMPLES OF "BADNESS"

People have the urge to be "fixers" instead of healers. When a child comes home crying after having had a fight with another little boy, his parents might be quick to offer a tender cuddle. But they also feel the impulse to make the situation better. Before they even realize it, they're suggesting how the interaction at school went awry ("Did you say you were sorry?"). They might offer ideas about how to think about the situation ("Don't take it too hard. Kyle is just teasing you because he's jealous!"). They might provide advice about how to behave differently the next time ("Just learn to laugh it off"). Or they may want to punch the other kid in the nose! But even the wisest, tried-and-true suggestions can create distance between caregivers and the person who's hurting. The words they use, their tone of voice, the mere suggestion that a problem is small and manageable can reveal the ways in which helpers are not *hearing* and *understanding* what's going on.

People do their most egregious "fixing" when they're advising others about their health. Everyone has a helpful answer. If a parent has high blood pressure, they suggest low-sodium foods. When a colleague groans about the aches of arthritis, they say, "Have you tried an anti-inflammatory like ibuprofen?" Recently, when one friend complained she had gained too much weight during pregnancy and that she was really worried about the way her body had changed, another quickly came to the rescue with the suggestion: "Can't you just walk a little bit every day?" No matter how good the intentions of the helper, the person who's hurting is seldom better off with these kinds of solutions.

Most importantly, the fix-it type of support offers only short-term solutions. The deeper, and sometimes long-standing, issue of what hurts still goes unaddressed. Instead of facilitating health, this kind of "help" actually prolongs pain and hinders recovery. When caregivers fail to acknowledge the big picture of another person's suffering, they fall short as friends, and they fail as supporters and helpers. Everyone wants to distract from anguish, but the real healing happens when caregivers help patients turn toward it and be with it.

Turning toward suffering doesn't sound like much fun. Who wants to do that? If I give a patient the option of getting a massage for the pain in his neck versus talking about the situation in his life that's *giving him a pain in the neck*, most likely he will choose the former. But the pain won't resolve until we turn toward the authentic cause. Both my patient and I need to give it our attention. As I explained in Chapter 2, this is the active process of facing what's really going on as compared to passively treating the problem with a drug or a massage. With an active process, the patient gets what he needs most . . . another's true presence. With that kind of attunement, life hurts less.

Over the years, I have found that people make many unhelpful statements that may rupture a connection, even though they believe they're doing their best to be present with someone who is hurting. In fact, most often, these comments and questions function as distancing devices. Here are a few familiar ones:

"I know what you're going through. When I broke my leg . . ." This is a form of narcissism. People turn the conversation back on themselves and their own problems as a way of "relating" to the other and "just trying to be helpful." How about: "When I had back pain, I read this book/did yoga/saw a chiropractor/had physical therapy/took narcotics/tried acupuncture, or you-name-it, and I avoided surgery." This implies that what worked for one person should work for another. Maybe, but maybe not. A patient's condition might be completely different, and others' well-meaning but misguided advice could actually worsen the problem. When people are busy talking about their own lives, they're not listening deeply to the other's pain so they're not really making a connection.

"You think that's bad?" This is the approach of instantly telling the person about someone else whose problems were worse as a way of diminishing what the injured party is suffering. As a good friend explained to me, "I can't tell you how many horror stories I heard about bicycling accidents after my husband took a serious spill that landed him in the hospital for a few days with 6 broken ribs, a bruised lung, and a face that looked like raw steak." Does anyone really want to add to the burden of the injured person and his or her family by sharing these one-upmanship tales? Whom do

they really serve? How are these stories helpful? And how do they reinforce the connection?

"Why are you telling me this? Can't you see how upset I am?" During a crisis or medical setback, family caregivers can become anxious and need to be taken care of themselves, diverting precious energy. This attitude also can cause the person they want to serve to conceal the seriousness of the problem or prevent him or her from reaching out for help when it's most needed—as a way of protecting *family members* from becoming too distraught.

"Snap out of it . . ." "Pull yourself together . . ." "It can't be that bad . . ." With this attitude, people communicate that they don't recognize the other's suffering or hardship. This heightens an individual's sense of aloneness just at the moment when support and connectedness are most needed.

"I'm so worried about you. I'm afraid you'll never get better." This may be the most destructive communication of all. If we convey confidence and positive emotions through our mirror neurons, which in turn can create a healing epigenetic environment and a reordering of brain cells, we can do just the opposite when we express doubt, fear, and despair.

WHAT HELPS

In The Healer's Art class, we ask our students to identify which statements or behaviors had been unhelpful when they were suffering a significant loss. But we also inquire: "What did someone say or do that helped you get through your challenging situation?" Consistently, others' simple caring presence and actions comforted them more than any advice did. Here are the most common on our list.

What helped? The other person:

- Just listened
- Cooked me some food
- Shared in and accepted my emotions
- Sat with me
- Gave me a hug
- Recognized my needs and didn't ignore or avoid me
- Was patient with me
- Was just there for me

People who are hurting need to be held and cared for. It is not knowledge, but rather presence and connection that count. They need to know that they're not alone in their predicament. "We'll get through this together," is a positive statement that conveys compassionate support and a willingness to be fully available. Perhaps this is why cancer support groups are so effective.

In the final analysis, I think it is important that caregivers do their best, but they will burn out if they believe they can change or fix people. It is more fun to be a friend and encourage through a caring connection. At least with this attitude, we will do no harm.

PART II

Make the Connection

6

Identify and Free Yourself of Your Biases

Everything that irritates us about others can lead us to an understanding of ourselves.

—CARL JUNG, *Memories, Dreams, Reflections*

In biological systems, everything is related. The most fascinating manifestation of this is how a nonphysical awareness, a thought, becomes a tangible chemical, a protein in the body. It all starts with the perception of information. Let's imagine a social worker is dealing with a "difficult" client named Joe, who causes her stress every time she encounters him. In the past, Joe had been argumentative and oppositional—thwarting all of her efforts to help him. What happens in Sheryl's body as she walks down the hall and catches a glimpse of this man in the waiting room?

The visual perception of Joe enters a back area of Sheryl's brain called the occipital lobe. That, combined with her previous experiences, causes her brain to make specific types of neuropeptides—brain proteins that affect the body. In this case, it produces a neuropeptide that triggers a stress response, which then starts a pervasive cascade of chemical reactions. One of the first is the creation of neuro-protein Y, which prompts her to crave sugar so she will have enough energy to "fight" Joe or "flee" from his presence. Her brain also triggers the secretion of corticotrophin releasing factor (CRP) from the hypothalamus, which travels down to the adrenal glands to start the flow of cortisol. Cortisol works by mobilizing sugar (glucose) to fuel her fighting or fleeing. It also causes weight gain. (If she doesn't fight or flee, this extra energy will be stored as fat for future challenges.)

Sheryl passes Joe with a nod and a timid smile, comments on the weather, and tells him she will be with him in a few minutes. She conceals her authentic feelings of dread as she returns to her desk and spreads cream cheese on the bagel she is now craving. But, because Joe is Sheryl's client, she cannot fight or flee. Instead, she stifles her emotions. The concomitant rise in the stress hormone cortisol raises her insulin levels, which increases fat deposits. This process, in turn, promotes inflammation in her body and the risk of disease. All this from an emotion prompted by earlier experiences with a client who Sheryl perceives as stressful. And now, she has to step outside her office and call Joe in for his consultation.

How can caregivers make a compassionate connection seamlessly even with difficult people, without stressing themselves and others to the point of burnout? How can they truly be of service? There are several positive steps to take in order to create the best connection possible—one that will help them genuinely be with the person who needs their help. Throughout the rest of this book, I outline these strategies. However, a true connection starts not with knowledge about the individual who needs help, but perhaps paradoxically, with a deeper understanding of oneself and one's biases that include reactions to stress and to others.

WHAT'S ON YOUR MIND?

Everyone has frustrations, prejudgments, and strong opinions accumulated from a lifetime of experiences. Those attitudes are imperative for guiding decision making and enabling people to interpret the world they live in, but they can also hamper close, personal interactions. In truth, and despite protests to the contrary, no one is ever genuinely objective. As diarist Anaïs Nin has astutely noted, "We all see life not as it is, but as we are."[1]

The reality in which individuals live is always a product of their own minds—their consciousness. As they gain information, whether from years of education or from hard-earned life experiences, their brains become conditioned, and in fact, closed off so that it is difficult to allow new realities to enter or change their opinions.

One study at Harvard conducted in 2013 made it clear how even highly educated and attuned professionals can become blinded to certainties that exist outside their well-honed frames of reference. In this experiment, attention researcher Trafton Drew asked twenty-four experienced radiologists to look at CT scans of the chest for tiny cancer nodules. He intentionally superimposed on the area of the upper left lung the image of a gorilla that was forty-eight times the size of the detail the radiologists were searching for. The experts carefully examined this altered scan, but amazingly, 83 percent of them missed the gorilla entirely, even though the picture was quite large. An eye-tracking device showed that they had gazed right at it, but clearly, the gorilla hadn't registered in their minds at all.[2]

How could this happen? Radiologists are looking for abnormal nodules that could be cancer. They know the shapes and characteristics of these lesions. To be as efficient as possible (in order to get through the stacks of charts and images they must read in a day), their minds home in on the configurations that trigger a "I-don't-want-to-miss-this" response. A gorilla image does not have these "red flags," so they ignore it and literally don't see what is right in front of them.

People notice what they are looking for, but because of their biases may miss important details they either believe are extraneous or fail to attend to altogether. The way most individuals have become conditioned to see the world makes them perceive their opinions as established "truths." But in the process of making a human connection, caregivers often must recognize that other people's experiences have shaped their unique points of view. If they intend to initiate a compassionate interaction with another human being, they first must understand their own biases, where they come from, and why they hold on to them. Most significantly, they must avoid projecting those beliefs (what I like to call clutter) inappropriately or too quickly on people whom they wish to help.

HOW BIASES CAN BE DANGEROUS

Recent research has shown that if physicians interpret their patients as disruptive or "difficult," not only do they experience negative emotions themselves but they may make inaccurate diagnoses, which can cause their patients harm. To test this theory, a research team in Holland created six scenarios that depicted patients as either difficult or neutral. Sixty-three residents in family practice were then asked to analyze these vignettes and make a quick or more deliberate diagnosis. The students also rated how likable the patients were. The results of this investigation showed that diagnostic accuracy was significantly diminished for patients who were deemed difficult as compared with those who appeared neutral. However, when the residents took the time to carefully reflect on the cases, the accuracy of their diagnoses improved, despite the patients' behaviors.[3]

A related study surmised that when patients are difficult, their physicians make mistakes because they spend mental energy on dealing with the disturbing behaviors, which impedes "adequate processing of clinical findings."[4] If clinicians prejudge patients as "difficult," this judgment (again, clutter) keeps them from accurately diagnosing the real problem. They start living in their own heads, which prevents them from seeing reality clearly. The truth is, no matter what the context, when we are nervous or upset, we make mistakes.

In a downward spiral, difficult patients may also trigger inappropriate behavior and job-related stress in the people charged with caring for them. For instance, another recent study investigated negative clinician behavior on their patients' outcomes and on the health of the clinicians themselves. When 1,559 clinicians working at an urban U.S. academic medical center were rude, disrespectful, self-centered or egocentric, gossipy, passive-aggressive, and even in the rare case, physically violent, not surprisingly they were likely to cause harm to their patients. But this was also associated with more physical symptoms in the clinicians and a greater degree of job dissatisfaction.[5] This dynamic is of particular concern in health care since professionals often work in teams. Unprofessional behaviors can affect not only the health of the patients being served and the clinician providing the care but they can also degrade the functioning of the whole team and by extension, the hospital they work in.

Biases—one's own internal clutter—can seep out and interfere with a positive, healing connection. I learned this the hard way, when my frustration led to a regrettable choice of words that could have caused more harm than good with my patient Bob. He was a genial man in his midfifties who happened to come from a well-off family. He and his wife, Anna, were empty-nesters. They lived in a nice part of town, dressed well, and enjoyed traveling. One of their greatest pleasures was dining together in fine restaurants, and they ate out quite a bit. But, while Anna sought out opportunities to hit the gym so she could work off those extra calories, Bob had always been quick to tell me that he hated gyms and disliked most types of exercise.

As a consequence, over the years Bob had gained quite a bit of weight—even to the point of being obese. He was aware of his girth and remorseful about it, but he hadn't managed to stop putting on the pounds. The weight gain had led to several health setbacks. He was now suffering from high blood pressure and worrisome cholesterol levels. In the previous year, he had also developed colon cancer. After finishing cancer treatment, he was back to see me in the office for regular checkups. We had completed his routine appointment, and we were talking about the importance of tests to check his blood glucose levels to ensure he was not developing diabetes. As we began to wrap up the visit, Bob sighed as he said to me, "Dave, when are they going to find a cure for obesity?"

Somehow his question hit a raw spot in me. Here I was sifting through ways for Bob to handle the physical toll of his lifestyle choices, which included his love of rich foods and his avoidance of exercise. I felt frustrated that he had not made any changes over the years to improve his situation. His colon cancer had been treated, but because of his weight, he was at higher than ordinary risk for recurrence. The complications of diabetes were right around the corner. It fit a pattern I was seeing in a lot of patients: an insatiable, never-ending desire to be taken care of, without any sense of owning their problems. It also fit a pattern of patients demanding a quick, silver-bullet fix to health issues, expressing impatience with doctors, never wanting to engage in the hard work of keeping themselves healthy. Where was Bob's sense of accountability? Why did he have no resolve or self-discipline to address his own predicament? Aren't we all responsible for taking care of the issues in our lives?

Bob's question touched on several of the long-standing

frustrations I've felt as a doctor—and as a person. Which may have been why the words that came out of my mouth next were less than compassionate. "They've already found the cure for obesity," I blurted. "It's move more and eat less!"

As soon as I had uttered these two short sentences, I wished that I could have taken them back. But it was too late. The look in Bob's eyes at that moment was one of hurt. I recognized at once that my glib comment had undermined my overall objective, which was not to shame or punish Bob but to help him find a way to address his weight issue.

I immediately realized that my judgment had been muddied by my own set of biases. I had allowed my frustrations (*Can't he see the magnitude of his problems, and that they're only going to get worse? He should know better! He never listens to me!*) to interfere with our interaction. Not only had I caused my patient unnecessary pain but I had missed an opportunity. Instead of providing an answer that could help Bob, I had forced my worldview on him, hoping he would suddenly see things *the way I wanted him to see them.*

If I had taken the time to answer appropriately, I might have said, "Sometimes simple changes like eating less red meat, white pasta, and rice or giving up soda (even diet soda) can make a big difference." But dietary changes work best (and patients are more likely to adhere to them) if the new regimen is their idea, their plan. So, if I wanted to maintain our connection, I might have offered words that would have enabled Bob to bring his own truths to the issue. For instance, I might have said, "Yes, that will be a great day, and I'm looking forward to it, too. But since we don't have that cure yet, what kinds of things do *you* feel are possible for *you* to do in the meantime, to bring about the changes you want so much?" If only I had thought to say these words to him then, I might have avoided such a negative reaction that clearly hurt my patient rather than helped him.

Once people acknowledge and separate their biases, once they get out of their own clutter, they can then access what they know to be of service to others. When they don't, they run the risk of becoming dogmatic and inflexible in their thinking. I fell victim to this kind of bias with Bob when I responded so unkindly to his wistful question about a cure for obesity. In my damaging interaction with him, I had jumped to apply my own viewpoint to his situation. I heaved into the conversation my professional perspective from medical journals, other members of my field, and my daily practice. These sources of information might have some factual substance, but they were not helpful to Bob. In the final analysis, at that moment of pique, I was unable to set aside my own preconceptions to truly be of service to my patient. In essence, I had enlisted the nocebo effect, and when I left the exam room, I felt terrible.

HOW PEOPLE DEVELOP BELIEF SYSTEMS

Research demonstrates that life experiences and the interpretation of information can cause physical changes in the body. Stress may manifest as elevated blood pressure, headaches, or literally, physical pain in various parts of the body. How does this happen? As I described in the beginning of this chapter, when we integrate information, we alter neuropeptides in our brains and engage the autonomic nervous system. Dr. Dan

Shapiro and I created a name for this conditioned response—the info-medical cycle (see figure),[6]—and I developed the diagram below to illustrate it, although the process is part of collective knowledge that has developed over time.

Fundamentally, the info-medical cycle looks like this: As people enter a new experience, they receive information. Their mind works hard to interpret the input in order to understand what they're seeing or the event in which they're involved. But along with that interpretation, they also have an emotional reaction that prompts a physiological response or physical symptoms. Those feelings—whether it's breaking out in a nervous sweat or experiencing the thrilling rush of joy—alter how they act. Ultimately, individuals base their behaviors on those feelings, and they store memories about them. Those experiences—and the changes in their bodies—help them form a belief system. The end result: the brain becomes accustomed to conditioned beliefs, and anything that threatens those beliefs feels foreign and makes people uncomfortable.

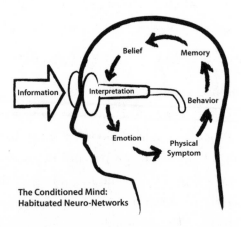

Even though the info-medical cycle is an inherent part of childhood, when every first experience is a potential source of learning and wonderment, people continue to reproduce this loop throughout their lives. When they encounter something for the first time, they don't respond with judgment or critical thought. The lack of judgment is sometimes called *looking through a child's eye* or as the Buddhists say, *having a beginner's mind*. People simply see things as they are and can register them authentically. As they gain experience and external input, they often lose the newness—the openness, vulnerability, and awe—of the beginner's mind. The positive aspect of growing up is that children eventually develop the ability to make beneficial decisions for themselves in this way. They seek situations that feel good and avoid those that feel bad.

But there's an inevitable drawback. As people go through life, they extrapolate from the experiences they've had. They revert to the *expert's mind* and come to believe their own established "truths" about the world. Although becoming "expert" might seem advantageous, in this context, the expert's mind is not a wholly positive attitude. It actually narrows vision and limits observations so that when new information is encountered, one can't help but apply the already established frame of reference, even if it doesn't fit.[7] Thus, the radiologists looked exclusively for cancer nodules in the altered CT scan and never even register the gorilla. It's so hard for people to relinquish closely held ideas and frameworks that Einstein once said, "Physics advances one death at a time."

BIAS AND NEURO-NETWORKS OF COMFORT

Imagine a picky eighteen-month-old who tastes a spicy burrito from his father's plate. The first time the child (Brian) is about to try something that's not on his ordinary menu, he's excited that he's doing what the "big kids" do, but he has no expectation about what he's going to taste. When the food enters his mouth, however, he finds it much hotter than what he's used to. His response to the spiciness leads to a bodily symptom: His mouth hurts, he sweats, and his heart rate rises. He bursts into tears. The event becomes ingrained in his neuro-network, creating a memory that he generalizes into a belief about the piquancy of all adult food.

The next time Brian's parents offer him something from their plates—say a bite of roasted chicken—he's wary. He sees the "information" differently now. Instead of feeling excited, he shuts his eyes and his mouth and shakes his head, "No!" His parents' food has become something he believes he *does not like.* Because of the release of neuropeptides that caused his bodily response to the chili peppers before, he may have some of the same reactions such as an elevated heart rate and crying—without even tasting the chicken. The memory of pain in his mouth leads to a behavior in which he refuses to try anything new.

All is not lost, however. Eventually, after sampling other foods, Brian will have positive eating experiences that broaden his palate and food choices.

I call a child's subsequent reactions to food after having eaten something that distresses him (or adult reactions to a previously painful event) the *habituated neuro-networks of comfort.* Life experiences create beliefs that start to feel normal. When this is reinforced, people begin to feel comfort. For instance, if a public speaker wants to give a talk that people will enjoy, she will tell them what they already believe. This conditioning process is neither right nor wrong. It's simply part of being human.

The trouble is that people don't always recognize the biases they hold from their accumulation of life experiences. Most importantly, they don't always identify them as *biases*, which is to say, they don't acknowledge that they're the result of perceptions and experiences, as opposed to truths. Biases can become as ingrained in personalities as breathing and are often referred to as implicit or unconscious bias. Unfortunately, they can impinge on interactions with others. In fact, the details of one's worldview can be so intrusive they may distort evidence that's plainly apparent.

One investigation, conducted in the 1970s and published in *Science*, showed that the professional biases of medical practitioners can cause them to diagnose illness even in people who aren't sick.[8] The study tested whether mental health professionals could pick out "fake" psychiatric patients. A group of eight research subjects, including a graduate student, three psychologists, a pediatrician, a psychiatrist, a housepainter, and a housewife signed on to become "pseudopatients" at psychiatric hospitals. Even though none of them had ever been treated for mental health issues, as part of the research project, each presented themselves at the front door of eight different psychiatric hospitals with a false name, complaining of hearing "thuds." At each site, the pseudopatient was immediately admitted, but soon after entering, he or she acted normally, displaying cooperative, pleasant, helpful behavior (as the researchers had previously instructed the study participants to do). When interviewed by psychiatrists, these individuals answered truthfully, providing accurate details from their own lives.

The pseudopatients underwent individual and group therapy and joined with the other residents in their activities. Because they'd been conditioned to do so, all of the medical staff believed the infiltrators suffered from schizophrenia. In other words, they regarded the pseudopatients as "sick" and even described their ordinary behaviors such as writing in a journal and walking the hallways as part of the illness. The pseudopatients were retained as inpatients for an average of nineteen days (one poor soul was discharged after fifty-four days!). For all of them, the discharge diagnosis was "schizophrenia in remission."

Significantly, the only people who detected that the research participants were not sick at all were the psychiatric patients in the hospitals who interacted with them as they ate, exercised, and attended group therapy. Not having had the professional training to view people according to particular pathologies or to fit a diagnosis, the people with schizophrenia were able to relate to the pseudopatients without labeling them. Using their beginner's eye instead of the goggles of professional training, the delusional patients with actual schizophrenia were the ones who were able to make the accurate diagnosis! The relationship they formed with the pseudopatients allowed them to see the latter authentically, as they truly were.

Meaningful interactions and the development of trusting

relationships reduce fear and are the remedy for bias and prejudice. This makes for a movie plot that writers can count on for good reviews. Here is the scenario. . . . A "different" person moves into town. This individual is foreign in a way that does not match the "norm" of the residents. Sometimes this fear of different causes people of the norm to treat the "stranger" badly, or even to do him or her harm. Different skin color, religious affiliations, cultures, or sexual preferences become the chosen label by which the norm identifies this new person who does not fit within their habituated neuro-networks of comfort. As the plot unfolds, out of necessity (for example, the need to overcome a common enemy, win the state basketball championship, preserve the town) the norm starts to develop a relationship with the different, and slowly trust and acceptance evolve. As the connection grows, there is less fear, and this new experience becomes part of a collective norm. Now different is no longer seen as a label of fear, but as a person, a friend, a helper, a coach, a teammate, a neighbor. This allows the diversity of the town to expand, widening the neuro-networks of comfort. The community is better for it due to the multiplicity of perspectives. The townspeople become less fearful of different and more open to the potential of what is.

Cue the Oscar music. . . .

EVERYDAY BIASES

When people adhere to the rote rhythms of the day, moving without stopping, they depend on the patterns and processes already established in their brains to help speed along their lives. They stop at red lights. They wait for the appropriate step to arrive when boarding an escalator. They check the size of a sweater before trying it on. But that dependence, helpful as it is, makes it difficult to observe the world anew from moment to moment.

The philosopher and father of psychology William James said, "Genius . . . means little more than the faculty of perceiving in an unhabitual way." Genius, maybe. But it's only through unhabitual seeing that caregivers can really bring their skills to bear in truly connecting with and helping others. To understand the brain's love of habit and pattern, take the following challenge. Read the sentence below once and count how many times the letter *f* appears:

FINISHED FILES ARE THE RESULT
OF YEARS OF SCIENTIFIC STUDY COMBINED
WITH THE EXPERIENCE OF YEARS.

It's an ordinary, dull sentence, and it's parsed in a way that's not particularly tricky. Most people looking for the letter *f* are quick to find three or four repetitions. Actually, it appears six times. Most miss the *f* each time the word "of" appears. Researchers have suggested several hypotheses to explain why those *f*s go undetected. For one, the word "of" is smaller than the others, and the eye may quickly skip over this minor consonant. In addition, when people hear the word "of" in their minds, the English-speaking brain is habituated to pronounce the sound of a *v*. It's possible readers miss the letter because it doesn't match the same sound pattern as the *f* in "finished" or "files." Whatever the reason, the effect is clear—the mind tends to perceive the letter without actually "seeing" it. The habits people have established in order to function in the world make it hard for them to discern important new details that are right in front of them.

People tend to approach their interactions with others in the same way. They look for behaviors and patterns they already know, placing strangers in categories they have previously defined. Fixed in their own biases, they might fail to seek out or perceive important details—for instance, a teary eye at the mention of a deceased family member or a physical tic that suggests discomfort. But in order to obtain the most authentic information so as to be of service, caregivers must first recognize how they view the world themselves. That means, they must acknowledge that they may not notice all the fs because of their mind's conditioning. Once they do, they can do a better job of looking through the other person's lenses, seeing them as they see themselves.

This was made clear to me when a school counselor described her experience meeting with an eleventh grader and his parents as the student transferred midyear into her high school. Melissa, relatively new to the job, quickly judged the Wilsons from their dress to be a white middle-class family. Working from that bias, she opened with several routine questions, asking sixteen-year-old Jeremy, "What prompted you to choose this school?"

With a dismissive shrug, he answered, "We just moved to the area."

Melissa continued to question the family. From her point of view, the meeting seemed to go smoothly. However, this point of view was based on her conditioned biases that kept her from seeing what was actually going on with the Wilsons. And this prevented her from making a correct assessment of the family's situation.

It was only later, upon further reflection, that Melissa realized her assumptions about the family were false. Jeremy had glanced at his parents before answering why he had chosen the school. His tone suggested a finality, a desire not to be asked anything more. Melissa later discovered that the Wilsons were homeless and were camped out in a shelter across town. Jeremy had no choice about which school he attended and was unhappy and embarrassed about their living situation. Melissa believed if she had clued in a little sooner, she might have looked beyond her biases and assumptions and established a better bond with him. That having happened, she might have observed his nonverbal communications more closely, and she certainly would have digressed from the standard questions on her list. Finally, she might have steered the conversation in such a way that she would have indicated to Jeremy that he could count on her as a supportive resource and ally.

Once caregivers understand their own biases, they can then try to see through the other person's lenses to make the most accurate needs assessment. However, if they fail to identify their own biases, just like Melissa, they can miss important opportunities. They run the risk of projecting what they believe onto the other person before they've had the chance to gather all of the information to be of real service. This projection can cause them to misconstrue a situation or misdiagnose a disorder or offer the wrong treatment—one that does not get at the root of healing. It may also push the other person into places he is not ready to go or leave him feeling unheard, invisible, and even unimportant. All of these emotions will rupture the connection.

It's easy to make the mistake of supporting one's own wishes and biases that don't serve the person in need. I've seen this painful situation among family members of dying relatives. For instance, some adult children who have not learned from their parent his or her final wishes want the doctors to do all they can to extend their parent's life, even when the prognosis is poor and treatment will worsen and lengthen suffering. This may occur because the children feel guilty for not having spent enough time with their parent, or perhaps they just don't know how to (or they don't want to) let go and say good-bye. They believe that they are acting for their parent's good. Unfortunately, however, they are operating out of their own biases and projections and are unable to step outside of them to really appreciate the best and most merciful course of action for their loved one.

One's internal clutter can have a pernicious effect on everyone. Social worker Sheryl's brief encounter with Joe caused her stress and eventual weight gain, and her reaction undermined her capacity to help him. She has the power to change this perception, but it takes work. She may need to recognize her reactivity and take responsibility—it might have caused her to identify in herself whom Joe reminded her of or what other issues she had projected onto him. Perhaps then she would have been more open and expressed to him her concerns or challenges. Maybe she needed to forgive a wrong he had done. No matter the process, it required that she turn toward Joe and connect in a way that would short circuit the same stress-related neuropeptide cascade the next time she saw him. And with this new frankness, it is possible that Joe could have revealed deeper insights about his life experience that would have helped Sheryl get beneath his crusty exterior so that she could truly be of service to him.

In some of the research I mentioned earlier, family medicine residents were more likely to make accurate diagnoses even with difficult patients when they took the time to deliberate on the cases. If caregivers never self-reflect, they may come to believe that everyone has the same habituated neuronetworks of comfort that they do. But after having been raised in a particular family and culture, every human being has been habituated to different beliefs. The good news is that once people recognize their biases, it gives them freedom to grow beyond them.

To be of service to others, it's fine to be comfortable in one's own beliefs, but caregivers must set them aside for the moment and transpose their perspective to appreciate another person's way of seeing the world. It allows them to convey their caring authentically. And it creates a more powerful healing effect because two people are vested in the outcome.

CREATING TRUST

It's easy to become mired in recurring mental processes or beliefs. But when people divert these habituated thoughts in a way that encourages them to see what's before them differently, they can have an epiphany that results in a new way of appreciating reality.

The power of communication is essential. Words can manifest a patient's potential toward positive or negative outcomes. One's intentions change perceptions. It all starts with caregivers' ability to recognize and set aside their own biases, to understand their universal connectedness, and to express their belief in the person. If they can create a strong bond, they are more likely to influence health outcomes for the good because they have forged a trusting relationship. I like to use the following equation, which I learned from The Napier Group, a management consulting firm based in Chester County, Pennsylvania, to define trust:

$$TRUST = \frac{INTIMACY \times COMPETENCY}{DEGREE\ OF\ RISK}$$

The higher the degree of risk, the more important the balance of competency and intimacy becomes. For instance, we might see a cardiologist who's at the top of her game, but who is cold and distant. Or we might engage one whose medical expertise is mediocre, but who is warm and friendly. In either case, our trust and care would be jeopardized. The latter may make us feel good, but we may not receive the best evidence-based care available, while the former gives us solid, up-to-date information, but leaves us feeling uncomfortable. In this case, we likely won't trust the physician or follow through on her recommendations. Moreover, the proposed therapy will likely be less effective because the detached clinician has not used the power of the connection to "stack the deck" in favor of the healing response. With the quick advancement of artificial intelligence, computers will be able to fill the gaps in competency, and human intimacy will dominate this equation.

The neuroplastic potential of the central nervous system can alter the neuropeptides that are generated with perception. A willingness to connect prompts an epigenetic influence in the caregiver that can create a healthy work environment or a dreaded one. In turn, a happier caregiver can shift her client's course toward healthier outcomes. And all of this derives from recognizing one's biases and stepping out of the clutter.

Ultimately, there's truth in Anaïs Nin's words: "We don't see things as they are; we see things as we are." To initiate a truly empathetic encounter, caregivers can heed the ancient Greek maxim: "Know thyself." It's also crucial to recognize how personal beliefs can potentially get in the way of healing. The better people understand the lenses through which they observe the world, the more clearly they're able to see beyond and around them as they prepare themselves to be a positive conduit in their interactions with others.

7

Be Present, on Purpose, without Judgment

All the qualities of your natural mind: peace, openness, relaxation, and clarity are present in your mind as it is.

—YONGEY MINGYUR RINPOCHE

My colleague, Katherine Bonus, is the founding teacher and past manager of the UW Health Mindfulness Program at the University of Wisconsin. With the permission of Gary's wife, she shared the following story about Gary, a young man in the end stages of cancer who had participated in her Mindfulness-Based Stress Reduction classes. Gary had asked Katherine to accompany him through his cancer treatment. She witnessed this interaction between him and his physician during his last hospitalization, about four days before he passed away:

Gary was 31 years old. He was experiencing his third recurrence of cancer, after having survived two prior diagnoses.

Chemo had sent him into remission twice before, but it was no longer effective. He was an enthusiastic human being, deeply loved and respected by his family and friends. Bright and successful as a graduate student and scientist, he was passionate about his work, in a loving relationship with his young wife, and eager to continue living. However, this third recurrence was not responding to treatment, and by the time this conversation took place, all medical avenues had been exhausted.

I arrived at Gary's hospital room that morning to find his wife in the hallway. She was visibly shaken and told me the doctor had just left after having told them there was nothing more to do. He was going to be discharged. Gary had sent her out to bring the doctor back, as he had more questions.

I entered the room and could feel the profound sadness and stillness that was present. The silence was tender. I waited quietly with Gary, his mother, and a friend for the physician to return. She entered the room and the conversation began again. "What about clinical trials? Gary asked. "There must be something else. . . . Surely there must be something more. Maybe something alternative?"

I watched the oncologist. Her gazed fixed on her patient. She was present, and kind. "There is nothing more we can do," she replied. "We've tried everything. You're 31, you're young. We want you to live. If there were anything else we could do, we would do it. Honestly, there is nothing else. I am so sorry." She paused. "Gary, you need to get out of this hospital," she went on. "Go home while you still have time and be with your family and friends. Turn all the energy you have about finding a cure toward your family. Have you said everything you want to say to them? Have they had a chance to be with you? I don't want you to miss this opportunity while you can. There isn't much time. Please, go home and turn your energy toward your family."

There was a breaking open with lots of tears in the room and then silence. Gary looked directly into her eyes and silently mouthed, "What happens when we die?"

She repeated the question as if to be sure that she heard it correctly. He nodded yes. She became quiet, took a deep breath, and seemed to drop deeply inside herself. I watched her. What followed I will remember for the rest of my life.

Her response came with such tender presence. *"I don't know what happens when we die. Some people believe there is a heaven. Some people believe we get to come back to life in a new way. I honestly don't know. But I do know this. Look around this room. You can feel the love that's here right now in this room. I believe you were conceived in love, you were raised in love, love is here right now, and I believe with all my heart, when you pass from this life, you will be received by love. It is love."*

I watched Gary lean back on his pillow with a calmness, an ease. There was sadness, and there was relief. She leaned over to him and hugged him. "Thank you for letting me take care of you," she said quietly. "I have loved caring for you. I want to say 'Goodbye.' Please, go home, live your days. I wish you well." With that tenderness, she left him.

The atmosphere of the room changed. Gary's young wife simply said, "Let's get you home." And together we began to make a plan. Gary was brought home that Thursday afternoon. He had the weekend with his family and some friends. Love was expressed; goodbyes happened. He died in the early morning hours of a Monday. He died in love.

I have no idea whether the oncologist practiced meditation. But I do know she was an embodied compassionate presence in the moment. She did not look away, avoid, or pretend. She had staying power to be with what was difficult. She had a steadiness of presence. She did not give well-rehearsed, contrived, automatic answers. She paused, listened, and met reality in present time.

I believe that through her presence she helped this man liberate himself so he could live fully while he was able to do so. Through her, he was more present to the reality of what is, rather than wasting his precious time. She paused, rested into stillness and clearly spoke from stillness. Her presence helped her patient and his family experience some peace in the midst of his real-life painful circumstances. It is said, "There is suffering and the relief of suffering." That's what I witnessed in that conversation.

A couple of weeks after Gary died, I wrote a letter to the oncologist thanking her for what I witnessed, for her true presence. She replied that when Gary had asked her the question, "What happens when we die?" she went totally blank. She felt deeply drawn inside, into nonthinking silence. It was as if the words came from silence, were spoken through her. She too had been deeply moved.

Mindfulness is the awareness that arises from being present, with heart, to what is, as it is. It is wisdom and compassion available to all. We practice simply dropping into our moments, one moment at a time, into the "isness" of life, letting go of fixed ideas and discovering the richness of the unfolding present moment. Mindfulness is not about getting rid of anything. It makes room for it all. It's paying attention to whatever is with kindness as best you can.

PAUSE AND BE PRESENT

In order to initiate an empathetic encounter, caregivers must drop into the moment with complete presence. The founder of today's mindfulness meditation movement, Jon Kabat-Zinn, teaches that this is like dropping a tennis ball into a hand. Although it sounds easy, this is no small accomplishment these days. People are interrupted and inundated with constant "noise"—Tweets, Facebook posts, texts, voice mails, e-mails, assimilating all kinds of information—only some of which is important or relevant. The mind often shuffles quickly among thoughts, sensations, and emotions. Minute to minute, caregivers find themselves pressured to perform, or impress others, read e-mails, follow current events, or even to get to their next appointment on time. All of this crowds the mind and forces people to mentally juggle the tasks in front of them, the last thing that was bothering them, and all of the stresses that await them later. I often visualize this endlessly churning mental activity as a tempestuous storm at sea.

Conversely, the state of being present is one that flows from the concerted, quiet effort of pausing. When people are fully present, their senses are alert. They're perceptive and open to details. They're prepared to take in information without judgment or analysis. True presence in the moment is in itself a communication to the person who is poised to listen. Being present, caregivers signal to their patient that they're offering their complete focus and attention. With their bodies, faces, and voices, they reveal availability. Just as the calm but alert martial arts expert seems adept at predicting a sparring partner's next move, the mindful clinician is able to move efficiently through a discussion, perceiving authentic signals that allow for the flow of insight and strategic action.

It's not easy to stay focused in this way—especially in life-or-death situations. For instance, had the oncologist responded to her dying patient's question with more information about the science of his condition, the outcome would have been much less effective for him and his family. Individuals don't remember what we tell them as much as how we made them feel. The oncologist's sensitive response addressed this man's fears, not the mechanics of his difficult situation.

Establishing a compassionate connection such as this one requires close attention, preparation, and thought. It demands pinpoint accuracy and emotional attunement. This is nearly impossible if the mind is perpetually in motion. The first step then, is to stop . . . to pause, as the oncologist did, to clear the mind of chaotic thoughts. This is when personal biases (one's internal clutter) can be identified and set aside so that one can be fully present and intentionally aware of the moment without judging the person being served.

It's important to resist the urge to hurry through a conversation, especially a difficult one, with a person who is suffering. It takes intention to keep the mind from wandering to distracting topics such as other patients or tonight's dinner. It takes self-awareness to avoid falling into ingrained beliefs and biases or responding in ways that are off-putting, unhelpful, or even damaging. Promoting salutogenesis is a deliberate act. The intentional behaviors of pausing and being present prepare caregivers internally to leave their comfort zone in order to consciously enter the space of the other's needs with a clear and open mind.

To do this, effective caregivers must first stop moving. They separate themselves from the cacophony of the world. They clear their minds. They let go of preconceived notions about their patients' lives and experiences. They drop into themselves, beneath all the internal and external noise around them. (This may require imagining that they are looking up from the seabed, observing the storm of thoughts and feelings above, but not getting swept up in them.) They pause to focus solely on the person in front of them.

Students are often surprised to discover that I mean this quite literally. A pause requires one to cease moving, take a deep breath, and remain in the present moment. It's important to know exactly when to be still during an interaction. Intimate connections are enhanced in these spaces of internal quietness. The power of the pause has been documented in a study published in the *Journal of the American Medical Association* during which researchers observed interactions between patients and physicians. They found that "nonverbal attunement" prompted doctors to stop moving and speaking at moments of heightened anxiety. When they were still, their patients often provided important information that they had hesitated to reveal. Conversely, if the doctors did not take time to stop, patients refrained from sharing valuable and vulnerable information. They held back, in fact, even when their physicians asked spot-on, appropriate questions.[1]

Most people, especially busy health care providers moving briskly from one patient visit to the next, are unaccustomed to *allowing* themselves the luxury of a pause. But even for harried doctors, this can happen in the hallway before entering an examination room. For me, it occurs when I place my hand on the doorknob. I stop and consciously take a cleansing breath before I enter and greet my next patient. A psychotherapist might pause between sessions to quiet the resounding echoes of one client before preparing for a conversation with the next. A manager might pause before calling an employee into a meeting about improving performance. A parent might pause before entering his teenager's room to discuss what he found under her bed.

The pause provides a moment's relief from the noise of the external world and from the incessant, intrusive, and often unnecessary whirring of one's own mental processes. It also allows caregivers to gain control over their mind's reflexes. In particular, it helps them break from the biases, the habitual way they process information, and the emotional reactivity that I discussed in the previous chapter. Once the critical mind starts up, people *feel less*, but for a connection to occur, it's important for them to *feel more*. It is for this reason that pausing is an essential element of compassion.

Induction for hypnosis and guided imagery requires a pause to get one's mind out of thought and into the place where suggestions will be more powerfully received. In fact, people pause naturally all the time—before hitting a golf ball or throwing a pitch or diving into a pool, before delivering the punch line of a joke, before posting an e-mail or letter. They pause and count to ten before reacting angrily or taking action. They pause before saying something significant that touches another's emotions. They pause before whispering a prayer. The pause invites meaning.

The process of pausing allows caregivers to halt the reflex that provides a snap judgment or prompts them to simply move on to the next routine question, living and seeing within the confines of their own mind's beliefs. It encourages them to observe with all of their senses. They can think before providing a prefabricated answer to the questions in front of them. There will be a time and place to bring in expertise, but to acquire authentic information that helps caregivers choose the most useful tools, they must first pause and see their patients as they truly are, and not through how they have been conditioned. As caregivers quiet their minds, they refresh the view and are better able to take in information they might have missed.

PAUSING, MINDFULNESS, AND THE COMPASSIONATE CONNECTION

Because the pause allows people to observe, without judgment, it is crucial to the development of a deep, empathic connection. But how does one foster the ability to do this naturally, seamlessly, and appropriately? From my experience, the practice of mindfulness is the key component of this important process. This is the capacity to focus on *one thing* on purpose, in the present moment, without judgment. This singularity can occur in many ways and through many different practices. The "one thing" can include the breath (pranayama yoga), the present moment (mindfulness meditation), a word or mantra (Transcendental Meditation), a prayer (religion), or a poem (the humanities). It can be an activity or even an extreme sport. When fly-fishing, the casting can be that "one thing" to focus on. And high-risk activities such as bungee jumping or skydiving can do wonders to focus the mind in the present moment. Perhaps that's why they're so addictive to some people. It makes them feel alive. It forces them into authentic living on purpose with nothing else on their mind but the free fall, or the base jump, or the inward two and a half somersault with a twist.

The practice is very simple. The mind will wander (as it always does), but then practitioners can gently bring attention back to their "one thing." This is also true when sitting with a patient, a friend, a family member, or a client. The connector can note without self-criticism the tendency for his or her mind to wander and then return to the person being cared for. In this way, that person becomes the meditative focus. In essence, one's work chair becomes one's meditation cushion.

One of the pioneers of using a mindful approach before engaging in medical interactions is Dr. Ronald Epstein, a professor of family medicine, psychiatry, oncology, and nursing at the University of Rochester Medical Center, in Rochester, New York. He is the author of the book *Attending*. In a classical examination of mindfulness among physicians that was published in the *Journal of the American Medical Association*, he found that the self-reflection inherent in this practice enables them to "listen attentively to patients' distress, recognize their own errors, refine their technical skills, make evidence-based decisions, and clarify their values so that they can act with compassion, technical competence, presence, and insight." Through mindfulness, one is afforded the capacity to pause, be present, and make a meaningful connection.[2]

Until I started to practice mindfulness meditation myself, I was unable to get my mind fully out of my own biases, busyness, and distractions. But the repeated act of pausing and focusing that occurs during this activity allowed my own mirror neurons to be more sensitive to others' feelings. I had rarely experienced this prior to having this kind of centering practice. In fact, it is so important, the University of Wisconsin School of Medicine and Public Health is now working mindfulness into the curriculum for its medical students and residents.[3] The University of Wisconsin integrative medicine program was also recently awarded a contract to teach mindfulness to clinicians throughout the Veterans Health Administration across the United States. The focus is on strategies to "change the conversation" from just attending to disease to taking into account "whole health"—from treating the illness to treating the *person*. This is shifting the culture of health care from a linear process (this disease is a result of a problem or behavior) to a circular process that helps patients realize they can transform and be empowered to find a better way and not simply be labeled as having another disease.

Encouraging caregivers to explore mindfulness within themselves will result in sustainable change in how they view the people they are caring for. One really needs to explore this self-reflective, philosophical journey before being able to provide it for others adequately. Caregivers can practice mindfulness in a two-minute encounter and in so doing can connect and develop trust even in very short bursts. Or they can stay in a mindful state for forty minutes or more. From our research, we have found that as we train our colleagues in this process, they improve efficiency and become better diagnosticians. What's more, their patients are happier with their care.[4]

THE BROADER BENEFITS OF MINDFULNESS

Other investigations have shown that mindfulness meditation actually has an impact on brain plasticity, reversing the negative emotions associated with burnout and strengthening resilience.[5] It can rewire brain circuits in a way that's healthful for mind and body.[6] At the University of Massachusetts Medical School, a team of neuroscientists analyzed MRI brain scans before and after intensive mindfulness training. They coupled this training with a few weeks of incorporating mindfulness practice during every-day activities such as walking the dog and washing the dishes. In a clear case of brain plasticity, the researchers found that the process of being aware and present in the moment increased gray matter in several regions of the brain, including those associated with stress management, mood, and sense of self.[7]

I found this to be true in research that my colleague Luke Fortney and I completed with the help of our talented mindfulness teachers in 2013 at the University of Wisconsin. In one study, we taught a group of burned-out, busy physicians how to practice mindfulness. We abbreviated an eight-week course into an intensive weekend class with two follow-up evening sessions. During these classes, we taught participants about mindfulness and the importance of pausing and being present, and how these practices influence interactions with patients. We followed these physicians' burnout levels and their stress, anxiety, and depression, and found that even though we didn't track whether they continued practicing mindfulness in the intervening interval, there was significant improvement in these measures over the ensuing nine months.[8]

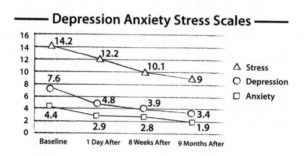

John Makransky at Boston College has tailored Tibetan mindfulness practices to be accessible to people of any faith or background. These meditations ease practitioners into "a state of simple presence and a compassionate connection with others." They provide sanctuary from inner turmoil and reactivity and restore energy. The mind relaxes and remains open—as Dr. Markransy puts it—a "profound letting be. That is where deepest rest and replenishment are found."[9] Practicing meditation allows people to feel as if they are dropping below the choppy waves of a raging sea into its calm depth. This is the place where one's innermost capacity of tranquility and wisdom is accessed. And it is from this place of calm that caregivers can best embody a sense of peace and safety for others.

Yet, for most people, this kind of serenity and focus is elusive. In November 2010, *Science* published an article entitled "A Wandering Mind Is an Unhappy Mind." The investigators, Matthew A. Killingsworth and Daniel T. Gilbert, wanted to discover how often people's minds wander, what topics they drift to, and whether those mental flights impact happiness. They asked volunteers to use a smartphone app that contacted them randomly during the day, asked them questions, and then recorded their answers in an online database. In 2010 this database contained nearly a quarter of a million samples from about 5,000 people who range in age from eighteen to eighty-eight and lived in eighty-three countries.

For their study, Killingsworth and Gilbert analyzed samples from 2,250 adults (58.8 percent male, 73.9 percent from the United States, with a mean age of thirty-four years). At random times of the day, the app contacted them and asked a happiness question ("How are you feeling right now?"), which they answered on a sliding scale from 0 (*very bad*) to 100 (*very good*). An activity question was posed ("What are you doing right now?"), which they answered by indicating one or more of twenty-two activities. Finally, they were asked a mind-wandering question ("Are you thinking about something other than what you're currently doing?"). They could answer this in one of four ways: (1) No; (2) Yes, something pleasant; (3) Yes, something neutral; or (4) Yes, something unpleasant.

Killingsworth and Gilbert then correlated these responses and discovered that people's minds wandered often (46.9 percent of the samples and in at least 30 percent of the samples taken during every activity except making love), regardless of what they were doing. The researchers found that the more the mind wandered, the unhappier the subjects were compared with those who were focused on one thing. This was true during all activities, including those that were the least enjoyable. Although minds were more likely to wander to pleasant topics (42.5 percent of samples) than unpleasant (26.5 percent of samples) or neutral (31 percent of samples) ones, people were no happier when thinking about pleasant topics than about their current activity and were considerably unhappier when thinking about neutral or unpleasant topics than about their current activity.

Killingsworth and Gilbert's analyses strongly suggested that the wandering mind they detected was generally the cause and not the result of unhappiness. They concluded that "the ability to think about what is not happening is a cognitive achievement that comes at an emotional cost."[10]

To me, the key here is that people are happiest when their minds focus on one thing well. But I always like to look at the extremes of the data. In this case, I wanted to know what the happiest people in this study were doing. It turns out that they were making love. This makes perfect sense, as it is difficult to have a satisfying sexual experience if one is worrying about tomorrow's presentation or replaying a recent argument with a sibling. In fact, one of the main causes of sexual dysfunction is the anxious, wandering mind, which can lead to erectile dysfunction and difficulties reaching orgasm. Consider a pleasurable sexual encounter. Two people are mutually giving and receiving, engaging in an intimate and reciprocal dialogue, focusing solely on each other in the moment. But immediately after the climax, what does the mind do? It jumps right into judgment. "How was that for you?" "Was it one of your top five orgasms of all time?" "Did I nibble on your ear long enough?" Being mindful, in the present moment without judgment, is the perfect recipe for good sex. But recognize how quickly one's consciousness wants to move on and jump to judgment and analysis—it always does.

Mindfulness is also one of the best ways to treat insomnia. Most people get great ideas right before falling asleep. In order to transition into sleep, the mind rests into one thought that evolves into no thoughts, and then, eventually, sleep. Counting sheep works on the same principle. Most sleep-induction insomnia is due to a racing, wandering mind. By focusing on "one thing"—the sheep—or engaging in a mindfulness practice (say, by beginning a slow and careful mental body scan starting with one's left big toe), extraneous thoughts disappear and relaxation and sleep ensue.

IT'S NO SECRET

On an intuitive level, most people are attuned to whether or not the person they're dealing with is connected to them and focusing on their real needs. Recently, I happened to overhear a conversation between two teenage girls that reinforced this for me. One said, "I'm done talking to her. I don't know why I bother. She never listens to me."

The other replied (rather absently, it seemed), "Really? I thought you guys talked all the time."

The first one said, "She always says, 'Yeah, that happened to me too.' And then she goes on and on. I'm done talking to her."

The speakers might have been all of fifteen years old, but

I thought their insights offered profound commentary about what's meaningful and what can go awry in an interpersonal interaction. Two people might talk "all the time"—in other words, have long-term interactions, general comfort about disclosing details, and a wealth of shared information about important experiences—but still the conversation doesn't *feel* complete or authentic.

Instinct kicks in and tells people when someone isn't fully present with them. The adolescent says she's sharing amply but still has the sense the listener (a parent? another friend? a sibling?) doesn't care deeply about the conversation. The fact is, just like in our common cold study, people know in their core when a connection is present or absent; compassion is there or it isn't. It's clear whether a person's words are being taken to heart, or whether a friend is only half-listening. Also, individuals can readily sense when they're respected as a listener as compared to when they're being talked *at* by a person who just needs another available pair of ears. Even though many words may pass between two people, they still may not make a real connection. What feels right in a conversation is having the opportunity to express an idea completely—from beginning to end.

Clients also need to sense that their caregivers got the point and didn't become derailed. We know from research that doctors can come up short in this regard. One study in the *Journal of the American Medical Association* showed that physicians tend to allow patients to speak for only twenty-three seconds before interrupting.[11] And then they direct the conversation toward a medical agenda that's not necessarily where their patients' concerns were heading.[12] Patients read and understand these cues.

That can be a huge problem in health care. We know from studies that patients who don't mention an issue and who don't ask their doctors for help are ultimately less satisfied with their care and experience less improvement of their symptoms. One investigation demonstrated that nearly 10 percent of patients left their doctor's offices with one or more unvoiced concern and were hesitant to ask for the help they sought.[13]

Multitasking is another modern-day issue that interferes with pausing and staying present. Would a person reveal meaningful information to a caregiver who is busily typing in an electronic medical record and not giving his or her full attention? I think not. The computer is becoming the primary object of focus in the exam room. It's used to organize a patient's information and help consolidate records within a system so that all professionals working with a patient have access to the same test results and diagnoses. That's all for the good. However, more strategically, it is also used to extract money, guaranteeing that the right codes are used to bill insurance companies. Typing on the computer differs from clinicians jotting notes on paper, which help them remember important aspects of a patient's unique story. Now they have to click buttons that have a right or a wrong pathway—with little space for gray areas. If they make an error, they must go back to correct it. When clinicians focus on the person, there is little right or wrong. There is only a story that puts a symptom into the context of the patient's life. The computer helps medical systems improve care in many ways, but it also interferes with the most vital aspect of care—pausing and focusing on what gives doctors the most important information . . . the person in front of them.[14]

Besides, the professional's level of distraction can be harmful. One of my colleagues, John Beasley, wrote a paper with Christine Sinsky entitled "Texting While Doctoring: A Patient Safety Hazard," which speaks to the value of being fully present.[15] "Texting while driving is associated with a 23-fold increase in risk for crashing and is illegal in most states," they write. "Using a cell phone while driving reduces the amount of brain activity devoted to driving by 31 percent. Multitasking is dangerous—cognitive scientists have shown that engaging in a secondary task disrupts primary task performance." And so they ask, "Might physicians typing into electronic health records pose similar risks?"

The sad answer is that they do. Multitasking can undermine important activities such as observation, communication, problem solving, and the development of trusting relationships. And this can interfere with proper diagnosis and treatment. John Beasley and Christine Sinsky have observed patients signaling depression, disagreement, or lack of understanding nonverbally and have witnessed "kind, compassionate, and well-intentioned physicians missing these signals while they multitasked."

In truth, when inputting information on patients' computerized records, physicians and others on a medical team devote much of their attention to the screen, not to the people they're helping. Even children are attuned to their divided attention. The *Journal of the American Medical Associa-*

tion recently published a drawing made by a young girl show-ing her doctor turned with his back to her as he input data into the computer. His complete separation is not lost on the girl. This reminds me of a story I heard recently from a dis-tracted father whose daughter asked him, "Listen to me with your eyes, Daddy." One possible solution to this problem is for medical groups to hire "scribes"—people who record impor-tant information during the office visit, allowing the physician to interact freely and fully with his or her patient. This, of course, can be costly and patients would have to agree to hav-ing a stranger in the examination room, but it's still a strategy worthy of consideration.

Most medical training involves some discussion with clinicians-to-be about how to develop rapport with patients. The word comes from the French *en rapport*, which means to be "in harmony with." Students even go through mock encounters with actors who play the role of patients. Those sessions teach the respectfulness of a clinical encounter. Students learn to ask general questions about patients' well-being and to present undirected conversation openers such as "What brings you in today?" Through these encounters they learn to take a history, conduct an exam, ask health questions, and even deliver bad news. Adding mindfulness training to this regimen enhances new doctors' relational skills.

There are also many subtle nonverbal aspects involved in developing rapport. Ultimately, the deepest, most meaning-ful conversation involves an interaction in which two people pause, drop down beneath the tumult, bring their individual selves, and work together to create something richer than the sum of the parts. Metaphorically, they enter a dance together. And, as you'll see in the following chapter, just as in a dance, in order to connect in a conversation, the first step involves establishing trust. All of that happens before anyone offers a single word.

NOT MISSING WHAT'S IMPORTANT

The state of pausing and being fully present opens one up to unexpected beauty. It might prompt creativity and insight. Caregivers could miss these moments if they don't take the time to recognize them. Of course, this is true of daily life, too.

I remember a day not too long ago with my family. We were on our way to Florida for a weeklong vacation, and the trip involved a connection between flights. Our first flight had been delayed, so when we landed, time was short to make it to the next terminal. We had our bags with us, and I kept checking my watch. I looked quickly at the arrivals/departures board to locate where we were headed. Urging my wife and children along, I began speed walking and then running through the airport, dodging other passengers, nervous about whether we'd make our connection on time.

Then I happened to look back. My wife and teenage kids had lagged behind. They were hurrying, but they were laughing, having a great time hustling through the airport. If I had not stopped in my determined route to get to the place I was certain we needed to be, I would have missed the delight in their faces.

163

So much of life is lived in the perception of the "what if." Our fretting yanks us out of the moment, into the stress of what may happen. But if we pause and are present, we can take in the beauty all around us, even while running through an airport to catch a plane.

8

Physically Communicate
Good Intentions

*Be solicitous in your approach to the patient, not with head
thrown back [arrogantly] or hesitantly with lowered glance,
but with head inclined slightly as the art demands.*

—Ancient Greek medical text, fourth century BC[1]

Some time ago, accompanying another physician in
a hospital, I observed an interaction that still stands out in my
mind. The patient was a woman in her thirties who had had a
history of drug use. Marcie was being seen for a heart problem,
which was not necessarily caused by her old drug habit (though
probably wasn't helped by it either). In recent years, she had
been taking medications for her heart condition, and she had
also been followed carefully by a team of doctors.

The cardiologist who was seeing Marcie that day assumed a
physical stance that surprised me. He greeted her kindly in her
hospital room, but as he spoke with her, he remained several

feet away from where she lay in her bed. When he asked her whether she had been taking her medications regularly, his arms remained folded over his chest. "What dosage are you taking?" he asked. "How many times a day?" Marcie answered dutifully that she had been taking all of her daily medicines at home before the hospitalization, and he nodded, posing additional queries. His questioning was thorough, and he reiterated how her prescriptions were helping her heart. But his stance and crossed arms conveyed something he might not have intended. *He doesn't trust her answers*, I thought. *He thinks she's lying.*

I didn't have the chance to discover after the encounter whether he really was concerned that she was exaggerating, but this physician's nonverbal communication had introduced the thought to me, and I'm sure Marcie must have picked up on it, too. If she felt he doubted her, would she be more or less inclined to tell the truth? Would she be more or less willing to take his advice? I wasn't so sure which way this would go. As the saying goes, "They may forget what you said, but they will never forget how you made them feel."

THE IMPORTANCE OF NONVERBAL COMMUNICATION

Nonverbal communication conveys authenticity more effectively than words do. It's good to know that a patient will forgive a poor choice of words if the caregiver takes a moment to pause and is present with authentic body language. Truth be told, I have said many stupid things that were quickly forgiven because my nonverbal communications were compassionate and superseded my words. Indeed, communication experts tell us that nonverbal cues carry more than four times the weight of verbal messages. Although the average person may command a vocabulary of 30,000–60,000 words, we humans rely on 750,000 nonverbal signals.[2] Not only that, scientists have found that we interpret nonverbal signals much more quickly and accurately than words.[3] Because this kind of communication is so prevalent and significant, in order to make a meaningful connection, caregivers must attend to and practice gestures that create resonance with another person and will allow a meaningful conversation to evolve.

The way people walk, sit, smile, and even hold their bodies can convey innumerable unconscious messages that either prompt a conversation or stop it cold. Imagine the difference in attentiveness caregivers can telegraph by keeping their bodies still as compared to impatiently tapping a foot or twiddling a pen. In fact, investigations have shown that if physicians sit down and get on the same level as their patients, the latter perceive that their doctors have spent much more time with them than if they actually spent twice as much time, but were standing with a hand on the doorknob.[4] They also perceived their doctor as more compassionate when they came down to their same body position.[5]

Research has even affirmed that simply the way people stand can have an effect on their body's chemistry and how they face challenges. Psychologists Dana Carney, Amy J. C. Cuddy, and Andy J. Yap tested this by comparing participants they'd placed in assertive poses, the kind of nonverbal communication you'd see in the boardroom, with those taking submissive stances, the kind you'd see in a doctor's waiting room. When they tested samples of the participants' saliva, they found that stances of power raise the level of testosterone and ultimately increased risk-taking behaviors, while at the same time lowering the stress hormone cortisol.[6] Their findings suggest that the way people hold themselves can change the way they feel and act, in part by influencing the hormones their bodies make. Certainly, posture can affect how people relate to one another.

Important silences, flushed or pale cheeks, abrupt changes of topic, or even momentary tears that are quickly blinked away are key indicators that all is not what it seems. If after asking a woman how many children she has, she answers joylessly, "Oh, two," as she gulps and her face reddens, those nonverbal cues must be heeded and probed. This kind of attention renders caregivers active listeners who hear an unspoken problem.[7] And, with patience and kindness, out may pour a tragic story of miscarriages and stillbirth or a child lost to illness or accident.

In this chapter, I present research about many aspects of nonverbal communication, including the effect of facial expression and direct eye contact, how posture can communicate good intentions, the power of touch, and the way gestures can reflect interest and affirmation. I also discuss techniques of posture, positioning, and mirroring that can help caregivers make a strong connection with the person they seek to help. Ultimately, they want to avoid showing the other person a "closed position," such as crossed arms, unintentional displays of boredom, or frustration. They want their physical presence to say, *I'm fully open to what you have to say.* And they also want to comprehend what the other person is conveying with his body as well as his words.

But before I dive in, I want to explain some of the subtleties of nonverbal communication to watch for.

UNDERSTANDING WHAT WE'RE SEEING

It has been said that body language is the unspoken truth.[8] But people must judge specific gestures in context. For instance, crossed arms could mean that an individual is being defensive, that he disagrees, or that he's feeling insecure. But it can also mean that his arms are comfortable in this position, or maybe he's cold. Caregivers must take into account what else is happening in an interaction to truly make sense of what they're seeing.

This means that individual gestures are significant only when considered within the context of a person's overall behavior. If verbal and nonverbal messages convey the same information, the communication is clear. A woman says she's happy: Her eyes light up, she smiles broadly, and she walks with a springy step—no problem. But when she says, "I'm fine," yet her sad eyes, shuffling gait, and drooping shoulders tell a different story, caregivers must pay attention to the latter. Even in the situation I observed at the hospital, although my colleague spoke kindly and sincerely to Marcie, because of his crossed arms and relative distance from her, I was unsure how his patient had received what he was saying. Unless nonverbal communications, words, and voice tone match, caregivers will be sending mixed messages that can confuse and ultimately distance them from the person they want to help.

Besides, individuals are quite adept at discerning what others really mean when they attempt to mask their feelings. People betray themselves with a thousand microscopic, unconscious clues. A finger to the side of the nose (Bill Clinton during the impeachment proceedings) or casting the eyes to the left if one is right-handed (is this why untrustworthy people are called "shifty" characters?) or speaking too loudly—can all indicate that someone is being less than truthful. Real emotions are likely to leak out despite one's best efforts.

If caregivers try to deceive the person they wish to help, by telling him he looks terrific when their nonverbal cues indicate that they're worried (being aware of the seriousness of the diagnosis), the patient is apt to mistrust them since he will resonate most strongly to the wrinkling forehead and downturned mouth, not to the words. Even if caregivers try to display a "brave front to cheer up someone," the person will recognize the insincerity, which can easily break a connection. This is all the more valid if caregivers attempt to hide from someone the true gravity of his situation with statements such as "Oh, you'll be fine" or "Next year, this will all seem like a bad dream." Most people read what's really going on . . . and others' attempts to smooth over the rough edges only serves to make them feel more alone, potentially activating the nocebo effect—the harm that occurs when a negative mind-set can be damaging if the interaction is inauthentic.

Whenever appropriate, caregivers must be congruent in their messages, sending the same information with their words and bodies. But what do those bodies say? And what about the bodies of the people they are charged with helping? Although it's impossible within the scope of this book to explore every nonverbal gesture, I will take a closer look at a few that can help caregivers make or ruin a good connection.

WHAT'S IN A FACE?

In *The Winter's Tale*, Shakespeare wrote, "I saw his heart in his face." When people first meet, they scan each other's faces for about three seconds to learn what they can—which is a lot. Studies have suggested that the human face is capable of seven thousand expressions (some have calculated as many as ten thousand), and when people interact, every countenance they make conveys their innermost thoughts.[9] When caregivers initiate a compassionate conversation, their interest and openness show first and foremost on their faces.

These expressions are understood the world over. Facial signs of pleasure, despair, and rage are no different among Australian aborigines than ranchers in Montana or fishermen in Norway.[10] Charles Darwin made this observation as long ago as 1872, after having collected input from missionaries who worked with native populations, individuals who were hypnotized, babies, people who were blind at birth, and those with mental illnesses. At that time, he postulated that all humans convey particular emotions with the same expressions. For instance, they usually show surprise by raising their eyebrows. People who were born blind and who there-

171

fore couldn't observe others, still raised their eyebrows when astonished.

A stony, nonexpressive face conveys that one is in command and powerful. Other facial expressions are the most immediately readable indicators that people are tender and nonjudgmental. As an extension of the pause, caregivers can relax any tension in their facial muscles to show they're ready to be responsive and prepared to pay attention. When they smile kindly and genuinely in greeting another person, they begin to build a connection. But they must control their expressions beyond that first moment. A furrowed brow, scowl, or pursed lips, for instance, may suggest preoccupation with other issues, or that they are already applying prejudgments. Darting eyes may send the message that they're waiting for something more to happen. A relaxed expression, however, says that they've dismissed other issues flitting through their minds. In addition, calmness in a facial expression says caregivers aren't about to impose their own agenda on the conversation. They're going to allow it to flow where it needs to go. With their faces, they've opened the opportunity for relatedness to begin.

However, paying attention to facial expressions can be particularly challenging in today's electronic environment. If caregivers are buried in their smartphones, or even just stop to check e-mails and texts during a conversation, they've taken their eyes and attention off the other person's face— and thereby broken the connection. Moreover, when inputting information on patients' computerized records, physicians and others on a medical team devote much of their attention to the screen, not to the people they're helping. That to which we give attention grows! So it behooves caregivers to become mindful of how their bodies convey their intentions and concerns.

The Eyes

One of my medical students failed an exam during which students interviewed mock patients to see how well they communicated, showed empathy, and developed trust. As he spoke with an older patient, Tom stubbornly avoided making eye contact. In his culture (Hmong), as in many others, it is a sign of disrespect to look an elder in the eye. But Tom's evaluation was based on the unspoken rules of our culture, and his demeanor was found to be deficient. According to the Western way of thinking, averting the eyes indicates a lack of connection and empathy. Thus, maybe inappropriately, Tom was judged to be lacking empathy. I worked with him on this aspect of nonverbal communication, retraining how he had been conditioned as a child, and eventually he passed this test. I'm happy to say that he became a successful resident.

Eye contact is quite complex and a key element of nonverbal communication. Forty different eyebrow positions express human feelings, as do twenty-three eyelid positions. (Imagine the many permutations that exist if we multiply these numbers together.) People can enhance a good connection when they maintain eye contact about 60–70 percent of the time. But that's just the average. If caregivers are good listeners, they make eye contact 80 percent of the time, but need only do so 40 percent if they're the one doing the talking. Indeed, frequent eye contact conveys sincerity. Ninety percent of the gaze focuses on the triangle created by the eyes and mouth.[11]

Where people place their gaze is also important. Rolling the eyes upward is unsettling and can indicate disinterest[12] or contempt. Downcast eyes can convey sadness or shame. If the person one wishes to help doesn't maintain eye contact but rather looks down or away, she may be shy or depressed, or she may be rejecting the caregiver or what he is saying. The eyes of anxious or stressed people involuntarily blink more often than those who are not so upset. Although the former may make eye contact as often as people who are less stressed, they hold the gaze for less time. This is especially true of people who are depressed. They maintain eye contact only 25 percent as long as people who are not depressed. At the same time, as Tom, my Hmong student, learned the hard way, those whom caregivers want to help may interpret minimal eye contact as a sign of stress or a negative response.

Even the pupils in the eyes matter. When they dilate, they indicate that people are seeing or experiencing something pleasurable, which they want to take in. The pupil dilates to let in more light, more of what they want to see. Conversely, when the pupils contract, it means people are dealing with some unpleasantness that they'd rather shut out. These reactions are entirely unconscious, yet they can still help caregivers understand someone's frame of mind. Indeed, this is why poker players wear sunglasses when they're at the table. The shades keep the other players from seeing the subtle pupil dilation that might reveal the winning hand.

As small a gesture as it may be, caregivers can convey many feelings with their eyes, including caring and compassion. In our culture, meeting another person's gaze and being willing to maintain eye contact (but not staring, which indicates hostility) begins building trust. It may seem merely like a pleasantry, as simple as greeting an individual by name, but in fact, these are acts that people remember.[13]

The Smile

Along with eye contact, smiles also convey what people are thinking. A smile reinforces friendliness, disarms a difficult situation, and promotes peace and safety—all to the good. I mentioned smiling kindly upon greeting someone, but often people also smile when they're uneasy or even anxious. Ethnologist Frans de Waal explains in *Peacemaking among Primates* that young rhesus monkeys grin when they're feeling threatened. "In social situations," de Waal writes, "the grin signals submission and fear; it is the most reliable indicator of low status among rhesus monkeys. In other species, such as humans and apes, this facial expression has evolved into the smile, a sign of appeasement and affiliation, although an element of nervousness remains."[14] Think of the third-grade teacher yelling, "And wipe that grin off your face!" after she finished reprimanding a student.

Authentic (or Duchenne) smiles are controlled by major facial muscles that connect to the corners of the mouth (the *zygomaticus major*) and the area encircling the eyes (the *orbicularis oculi*). According to Guillaume Benjamin Amand Duchenne, the French neurologist who first published these discoveries in 1862, when these eye muscles contract, the cheeks lift, the skin under the lower eyelids puckers, and wrinkles appear at the outer corners of the eyes.[15] This is a genuine smile. However, at a party or other social gathering, individuals can (and often do) fashion their mouths into a broad, fake smile at will, even if they're feeling unhappy or angry. Indeed, in our culture, people—especially those who are depressed or sad—will hide their true feelings by smiling. When observed sharply, one might detect a false smile because the eyebrows, eyes, and forehead don't move much. That's where to look to really understand a person's emotional state.

The crinkling of the muscles around the eyes (creating crow's feet) when people truly smile is unconscious and is hard to be willed into existence. Most people can distinguish a false from a genuine smile. The latter lights up the face and eyes, indicating enjoyment, while the former shows mostly on the mouth and is more likely to be perceived as an attempt at deception.[16] Before considering Botox injections to erase crow's feet, people should remember that those wrinkles inform others of their sincerity and genuine pleasure. Without them, faces appear too plastic and are unable to convey one's true emotional state.

Delivering bad news may render clinicians anxious. However, softening the blow with a false smile can send a mixed message that's both confusing and off-putting. So it's helpful for caregivers to be mindful of their smiles if they find themselves in this difficult situation. Otherwise, the connection they're trying so hard to build may rupture for reasons that may feel mysterious to them.

HAND AND ARM GESTURES

People may begin an encounter with a handshake, which in bygone times revealed a weaponless hand, and remains in many cultures a sign of respect and mutual agreement. A compassionate handshake generally involves a firm grip that conveys confidence (one's own self-respect will reflect back to the individual) but isn't arrogantly strong or overbearing. It's softened with kind eyes. A tender addition to the handshake may be a touch with the left hand on the other person's right elbow or covering their right hand with one's left during the encounter. These signals of warmth at the right moment can be as welcoming as a smile. The dominant person usually takes the top position during a handshake. If caregivers want the client to feel more confident, it's easy to roll their hand under so that the client's hand is on top. But ideally both hands are equally vertical.

Caregivers should observe the resting hands of the person they want to help. If they lay limp and floppy in her lap, she may be sad or have low self-esteem. Fidgetiness or grasping behaviors can show anxiety, as can shakiness or twitching. The white-knuckles of a clenched fist can conceal anxiety or anger. But palms turned up and out can denote warmth and openness.[17]

The patient may use her hands to indicate that she wants to interject her ideas into a conversation. To do so, she may create a steeple in front of her face by touching the tips of her fingers to each other. Steepling suggests that she has something important to say and can signify self-assurance. Or she may raise her hand or simply an index finger slightly to indicate that she wants to speak. On the other hand, if she places that same finger on her lips (as if to say, "Shh!"), she may be trying to keep her ideas to herself. In that case, a caregiver may want to probe a bit further to see what's on her mind, or he may wish to explain himself more clearly.[18]

If someone has folded her arms, she may be signaling a "closed" attitude. In effect, her arms are creating a physical barrier to the situation or information she's receiving. People also use this stance when they're bored or expectant or are braced for displeasure. Some people say of crossed arms, "I just do it because it's comfortable." But as was evident in the conversation between Marcie and her physician, this nonverbal cue can also communicate *I am not fully open to what you have to say.* However, if a person's arms are so tightly crossed that she seems to be hugging herself, she may be feeling insecure or sad and could benefit from being comforted.

POSITION

When people are seated, they signal their interest and engagement by sitting tall and leaning just a little bit forward. On the other hand, leaning back can make them seem less interested and even complacent. Sitting rigidly erect indicates tension— also not the best position to take when making a connection. And too much of a forward angle can seem aggressive—as if someone were encroaching in an overbearing way. Personal space differs by culture. In the United States, it is two to three feet—basically an arm's length. For others it is much tighter.

Caregivers should not move closer to someone than what's acceptable until they're invited into the other person's space, even when seated.

In addition, when caregivers initiate a compassionate conversation, they must make sure they are positioned at a similar level to the person they're caring for. Seating arrangements that place one person higher than the other can suggest the presence of hierarchy or privilege and can instantly be off-putting. For instance, if a doctor is standing, conducting the conversation while looking down on a patient who is sitting or stretched out on an examination table, the patient may feel diminished. It's hardly a way to make a person feel empowered.

Similarly, a parent who wants an honest answer from his teenager about whether drinking is taking place at parties would do well to sit down with the teen face-to-face. Having a conversation on the same physical plane doesn't make the father and child peers—there's still an imbalance of responsibility and authority—but the physical position helps ease a dynamic of blamefulness and defensiveness, enabling a more productive conversation to ensue.

TOUCH

Some experts in nonverbal communication consider touch to be the master sense—underlying all others. Think about it. We taste something when it touches our tongue, hear something when sound waves touch our ear drums, and see something when images touch our retinas. Indeed, touch has been called the most influential nonverbal communicator of all.[19] It can change the meaning of words almost instantly, even if the utterances seem unimportant.

Beneath awareness, the skin can send and receive information that is quite important. One research study showed that waitresses who touched their customers for *less than a second* on the shoulder or hand when returning change or the credit card slip received larger tips than those who refrained from physical contact with their customers.[20] In another investigation, students whom college librarians grazed briefly on the hand at checkout rated the quality of the library much more highly than a control group that received no such touch.[21] And many studies of preterm babies in the NICU who are held skin to skin on their parents' chests and gently stroked clearly establish that these infants need fewer interventions, recover much more quickly from the effects of their prematurity, and leave the hospital sooner.[22]

When touch is included in the medical encounter, patients perceive their appointments as longer and more positive than they actually are. If I'm in a hurry and the situation does not demand a long visit, I will still try to incorporate touch into the therapeutic ritual. This is why the physical exam is so important, even if I feel the presenting complaint doesn't warrant it.

While other cultures may condone frequent cheek kissing, hand-holding, and hugging, in the United States there are many unspoken rules about when and where to make contact. Touch communicates a wide spectrum of feelings from antagonism and anger to comfort and love, and the same behavior can have many meanings depending on its context, duration, and intensity; the toucher's intent; and where on the body the contact occurs. For instance, it would be perfectly acceptable for a mother to tuck in her young son's shirttails, but she would be awfully upset if a stranger attempted to tidy him up in this way.

Many professionals touch the people with whom they interact every single day—say a nurse or manicurist or dental hygienist. This has been called "cold touch" since in most instances, not much emotion is conveyed. These individuals are simply doing their jobs, which involve physical contact. Shaking a colleague's hand or tapping a woman on the arm to indicate that her purse has opened or that the bank teller is ready to receive her is called social-polite touching. People do this all the time with acquaintances. It's relatively anonymous, in contrast to touch that indicates friendship and warmth. That's when a person puts an arm around a friend, hugs, or otherwise physically reassures someone close to them. The most intense kinds of touch involve intimacy and love—caressing, kissing, holding, cuddling. These behaviors soothe, bring comfort, and elicit the release of oxytocin.

As a physician, I am required to touch my patients, palpating an abdomen or feeling around the throat for the thyroid gland, for example, when I perform a physical. But I also consciously touch them when I listen to their heart. In one hand, I hold the stethoscope to their chest, but I place the other on their back, creating a type of hug. This is much more than just listening to the heart. I am taking them into my hands and conveying that I am there to support and care for them.

If caregivers are not in an intimate relationship with someone but still want to offer a reassuring or comforting touch while helping them, the safest spots are on the outside edges of their body: the back, shoulder, outside of the arm or leg (when seated). And although helpers may believe that everyone needs a hug, it's important to note that hugs don't always heal. Some people feel uncomfortable with close physical contact. Pushing it on them can undermine trust and connection. Or they may have some medical reason that would obviate a squeeze. I learned this the hard way when I hugged a colleague who, it turns out, had severe arthritis in her shoulders. My friendly embrace caused her undue pain. It's best to learn about the person's unique situation and ask if it's all right to hug before making a move.

MIRRORING

When synchronizing two engines, one changes its speed to come into rhythm with the other. The same can be true of the brain. Perhaps due to mirror neurons, two people can fall into step with each other, mimicking each other's feelings and non-verbal signs. Not all of this is unconscious. "Body mirroring" is a behavior that can be learned. In fact, many business books provide chapters on how and when to do this. Everyone from the CEO to salespeople are familiar with using their bodies to win over potential clients. I can assure you that drug reps are quite adept at this. The idea is to take on the other person's nonverbal communication—without calling attention to the gestures—in order to convey respect and establish trust.

Ultimately, earning "respect" in sales gets someone to buy what salespeople are selling. But in the compassionate encounter, caregivers mirror nonverbal communication to put patients at ease and to show that they're ready to meet them where they are. If the patient slouches, the caregiver might partially slouch, too. His slouch says, "I see you're low, and I feel your pain."

When mirroring in this way, the caregiver's body helps create resonance or rapport with the other person; it's an important way to forge a connection.

Clinicians can also lead or guide with their own bodies to help someone open up and share valuable information. They start by mirroring a patient's body language and developing trust with the eyes and subtle caring expressions on the face. Then, once the connection is started, they slowly unfold their bodies to a more open position in hopes that the other person will follow suit. Here is how this might work: If the patient is sitting in a closed position—for example, arms folded over the chest and legs crossed—the caregiver would imitate his stance. Next, the caregiver would model a more relaxed version of this position with loosely crossed arms and legs. This posture is less defensive and indicates availability. Then, the caregiver would uncross his or her legs entirely and lean forward to show engagement. Finally, the patient's new openness would telegraph that he is comfortable and ready to share.

Nonverbal communication is not simply a mirror but part of an evolving yet subtle dance. Caregivers hope their bodies prompt in the speaker that fundamental instinct that, yes, the conversation *feels* right, and that any words yet to be spoken will be well received.

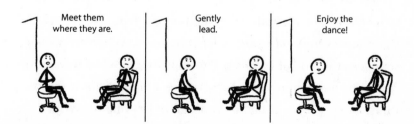

Meet them where they are. Gently lead. Enjoy the dance!

On the other hand, when the patient moves in such a way that he disrupts the mirrored position, he may be indicating discomfort, disagreement, or a sense of betrayal that he can't (or won't) put into words. If caregivers notice this disconnect, it would be wise to address what might have prompted it.

HOW TO TELL WHETHER SOMEONE IS LYING

Other nonverbal behavior communicates that an individual is shading the truth or outright lying. For instance, I might ask a patient whether he is ready to stop smoking. He may tell me that he is, but his nonverbal cues indicate to me that he isn't. I can deduce this even before he answers because he has used what's called the respiratory avoidance response. He coughs as if to clear something from his throat even though there's nothing there. This behavior generally suggests that he is uncomfortable with what he's saying.

Or he may put his finger to his nose the way Johnny Carson, one of the early hosts of *The Tonight Show*, used to do before telling a risqué joke. This is not the vigorous rub a person would use to scratch an itchy nose but a few gentle strokes or flicks. Some experts believe this is "a reflection of the fact that a split is being forced between inner thoughts and outward action."[23] As mentioned earlier, while Bill Clinton testified before a grand jury, he touched his nose infrequently when he was truthful, but he did so twenty-six times when he lied.[24] Someone who tugs an earlobe, scratches the side of his neck, rubs one eye, blinks to excess, or smiles for too long (most natural smiles last only four or five seconds) can also be stifling his emotions or shading the truth.

If caregivers notice these behaviors accompanying a "Fine!" in answer to their question, "How are you doing?" they can follow up with an open-ended comment such as "Really?" or "Tell me more."

PUTTING IT ALL TOGETHER

A patient's first contact with his or her caregivers is key. It is where the patient will perceive whom the caregivers are and whether they will be a good fit. The interactions following that first impression will provide the patient with information needed to confirm his or her intuition.

Additional strategies may help make the right first impression—one that can lead to a strong connection. For instance, caregivers should read the patient's energy and react in a way that shows respect. If someone engages, they should convey a message through the eyes that they are available and have their full attention. If appropriate, caregivers can also touch the patient in some way. This is generally a handshake, but it may also be a gentle touch on the shoulder. They should mirror the patient's body language and then slowly lead him or her to an open and trusting position, as indicated above.

The pause should be utilized appropriately if caregivers note an emotion that warrants further exploration. For instance, if a patient's eyes slightly well up when asked about marriage, caregivers should stop, show concern, and gently pursue the emotion with a question such as "When I asked about your relationship, I saw that a tear came to your eye" [. . . Pause] or "If that one tear could speak, what would it want to say?" In this regard, it's important to watch for consistency between body language and words. If there is a disparity, gently explore further.

If a patient doesn't participate in the therapeutic dance (he or she doesn't partake in mirroring, for instance), caregivers should not force the issue, as this will upset the individual. Rather, with words and nonverbal cues, they can show caring, and perhaps the person will be more open the next time they meet.

When someone is willing to partake in the dance of connection, enjoy it! This is one of the most rewarding interactions caregivers can have. And once two people connect, it creates a chemical reaction. Both are transformed!

9

Seek Another Person's Authentic Story

The most precious gift we can offer others is our presence. When mindfulness embraces those we love, they will bloom like flowers.

—THICH NHAT HANH, *Living Buddha, Living Christ*[1]

"Since communication is the glue that holds individuals together in society, I cannot but wonder whether society would run better if communication worked better."[2] So said George A. Miller, president of the American Psychological Association in 1969 in a statement that is as true today as it was then. How can communication "work better," especially among caregivers and patients where the stakes are so high? It is a truism that there are two sides to every story: the side of the person who is speaking and that of the listener. The aim, when making a true connection, is for there to be as little distance as possible between these two poles—that is, ideally, what the speaker conveys is absorbed, understood, and acted upon by the person to whom the story is told. Sir William Osler has said, "It is more important to know what sort of person has a disease than to know what sort of disease a person has." To really know the sort of person caregivers are dealing with, they must converse with him about his truths.

This seems an easy goal, but unfortunately, all too often, caregivers fall short. As we've seen, unless one is vigilant and mindful, biases and internal clutter can cloud the interaction. And then there are times when a "duologue" rather than a dialogue occurs. This is when people are talking at each other rather than with each other—everyone speaks but nobody listens. Duologue is monologue waiting its turn. Dialogue, on the other hand, denotes *meaning running through*.

A case in point: Recently, Dr. Michael Stein, an internist and the chair of Health Law, Policy and Management at Boston University, described in the *Washington Post* how the gap between speaker and listener widened to a chasm for his friend Sophia when she realized that something was "seriously off" with her health and sought help for neck pain and a low-grade fever from an unseasoned physician at a walk-in clinic. Here is how Sophia, who admitted that she rarely visits doctors, described the encounter:

"Would you test me for strep?" I ask.

"You're overreacting. You just have a cold," this young doctor says.

Would he have liked to hear me make a bigger deal about how badly I felt? I almost had to beg for the strep test. When it comes back positive, I'm so angry, I can barely speak to him. He was incompetent. Or trying to save money. Or maybe he was just lazy. He was certainly unkind.

Sophia's young doctor failed her in many ways. His poor bedside manner was matched only by his lack of skillfulness as a diagnostician. But, perhaps most importantly, he violated Sir William Osler's dictum: *Listen to your patient; he is telling you the diagnosis.* I also found it interesting that the word "unkind" remained in Dr. Stein's mind for weeks after he'd heard this story.[3] Isn't that what we all seek from caregivers—compassion and kindness?

Failures in communication such as this one not only hurt patients emotionally but they can also be quite costly physically and fiscally. CRICO Strategies, a research and analysis offshoot of the company that insures Harvard-affiliated hospitals and has a robust data bank compiling approximately 30 percent of U.S. malpractice cases, released a report in 2015 that analyzed more than twenty-three thousand medical malpractice claims and suits in which patients suffered some degree of harm; three out of every ten cases include at least one specific breakdown in communication in which facts, figures, or findings got lost between the individuals who had that information and those who needed it—across a wide spectrum of health care services and settings.[4] Hospitals and doctors' offices nationwide might have avoided 1,744 patient deaths and $1.7 billion in malpractice costs if medical staff and patients had communicated better. These failures to connect involved medical horror stories that no family or professional wants to experience.[5] Caregivers' ineptitude at communicating is largely to blame for the United States' $3 trillion health care system that results in poorer outcomes when compared with other countries that spend far less on their patients.[6]

The consequences of poor communication may be disastrous for everyone. How can people avoid these devastating scenarios? The benefits of trust and open sharing on the part of the speaker and what I like to call *deep* listening on the part of the receiver are manifold. There is no downside. Indeed, when these activities occur in the context of a medical visit or other salutary encounter, not only are grave mistakes avoided but health and well-being can actually be improved. So let's look at both sides of the story.

THE THERAPEUTIC VALUE OF TELLING ONE'S AUTHENTIC STORY

I knew Monica to be a kind, joyful person—one who giggled often. She was in her late seventies and had been diagnosed with the common but dangerous trilogy of diabetes, elevated cholesterol, and hypertension. During one of her office visits, I noted that her blood sugars and blood pressure were spiking somewhat alarmingly. Had I not invoked my connection with my patient, I might have lectured her on the dangers of her lifestyle choices and urged her to adhere more closely to her diet and exercise regimen. Or I might have increased the dosages of her medications—probably the most efficient action to take. However, I also knew that this status change among diabetes patients is frequently a reaction to stress. So instead of exhibiting a more authoritarian attitude, I paused and took a breath. Then, I simply asked Monica, "What's new in your life these days?" When she started talking about her son, I noticed her gaze fell to her lap. Her eyes filled, as if she were about to cry. Her nonverbal behavior prompted me to gently inquire further.

It was difficult for her, but through her tears Monica eventually revealed that her son was acting abusively toward her. I remained silent as she poured out her heart, but I watched her face and listened intently to her words and intonation. I was honored that she was willing to share with me the story of someone whom she loved but who was treating her so badly. Because of the underlying trust between us, she felt safe in conveying a truth that felt shameful to her. And that helped me better understand the effect this situation was having on her emotionally and physically.

When she reached the end of her story, Monica seemed peaceful. Indeed, because our interaction provided her the space to unburden herself, she left my office in a more cheerful state. And over time, her health improved as her sugar and blood pressure markers diminished to less dangerous levels.

My experience with Monica provides valuable lessons. First, people are unlikely to speak their truth or express their genuine emotions unless they feel safe and perceive the listener as trustworthy and caring. Without these structures in place, their words will be shallow, meaningless blather—and their well-being will be undermined. This has been borne out in scientific investigations. For instance, Matthias Mehl asked nearly eighty students to wear electronically activated digital audio recorders that unobtrusively tracked their conversations over four days. He then correlated the students' well-being and "happiness" with their engaging in less small talk (uninvolved, banal chatter) and more substantive, involved conversations in which meaningful information was exchanged.[7] These deeper conversations do matter.

But perhaps even more importantly for our purposes, if people don't share significant truths, valuable healing opportunities will be lost. Research has consistently documented that talking or writing about emotionally upsetting experiences has physiological benefits. It has been found that meaningful interactions improve physical health over time (as was evident in Monica's case), enhance immune function, and result in fewer visits to medical practitioners.[8]

Social psychologist James Pennebaker has studied the health consequences of keeping secrets, expressive journal writing, and natural language. A pioneer in the field of writing and narrative therapy, he has researched the link between language and recovery from trauma. He and his colleagues developed a computerized text analysis program called the Linguistic Inquiry and Word Count that analyzes eighty linguistic categories of speech such as the use of pronouns (whether a person uses "I" or "we," for instance); psychologically weighted words expressing primary negative affect such as "anger," "fear," or "sadness"; and particular topics like relaxation or money. His work builds on previous research establishing strong links between a person's speech patterns and his or her personality or psychological state. Pennebaker and his teams have used this tool to analyze people as disparate as Al Qaeda operatives and U.S. presidential candidates.

In one of his early studies, Pennebaker and his team interviewed polygraphists (operators of lie detectors) who worked for the FBI and the CIA. In performing these tests, the polygraphists would look for changes in their subjects' autonomic nervous system responses such as heart and respiratory rates, blood pressure, and skin conductance (the amount of sweat leaking into their skin) for clues of whether they were telling the truth. Pennebaker and his team found, in what he dubbed the "polygraph confession effect," that readings in these areas dropped significantly after a person confessed. These changes are consistent with those seen when a person relaxes.[9]

Holding in negative emotions and keeping secrets takes a physiological toll. Investigators believe that actively inhibiting thoughts, feelings, and behaviors requires physical work that results in chronic low-grade stress on the autonomic nervous system, which may then lead to or worsen disease. This inhibition can also trigger dysregulation of the hypothalamic-pituitary-adrenal axis, causing elevations in the stress hormone cortisol that are usually accompanied by weight gain and immune suppression.[10]

How does this work? Disclosing stressful events transfers difficult repressed thoughts from the unconscious to a conscious level where people can better organize and control them. Talking about these occurrences allows the mind to interpret this previously hidden information and unlocks emotions that can stimulate positive physiological results. It removes the need for chronic low-grade stress to stimulate the autonomic nervous system and the hypothalamic-pituitary-adrenal axis, which can cause a cascade of chemicals and hormones that lead to stress-related symptoms and poorer health outcomes.[11]

Examples from the aftermath of 9/11 elucidate how this phenomenon actually occurs. Shortly after the destruction of the World Trade Center, James Pennebaker's team researched New York City residents' online journal entries two months before and two months after the attacks. They found that the New Yorkers switched in their writings from more egocentric first-person singular pronouns ("I" and "me") to more communal words that foster relationships such as first-person plural pronouns ("we" and "us"). It seems that this tragedy opened these people to heighten their connections with other members of their community.[12] Most interestingly, Pennebaker correlated these findings with visits to health care providers and found that as the people of New York shared more, they made fewer doctor visits during the difficult postattack period.

This kind of openness takes place naturally for two or three weeks after a tragedy. During this emergency phase, individuals and the media discuss the event frankly. But after about three weeks, conversations decrease, despite the fact that feelings and thoughts have not diminished. This is called the inhibition phase. Research has found that journaling and talking can be most beneficial during this stage when expression wanes but thoughts remain.[13]

Numerous studies have investigated the positive impact of emotional disclosure (in written or oral form) on the experience of trauma, pain, and also particular health conditions such as asthma, rheumatoid arthritis, fibromyalgia, wound healing, and irritable bowel syndrome. In one study that involved 107

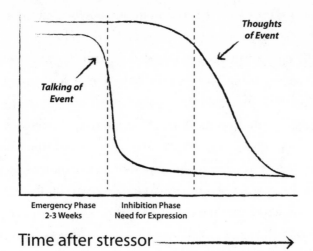

Talking of
Event

Thoughts
of Event

Emergency Phase   Inhibition Phase
2-3 Weeks   Need for Expression

Time after stressor ——————→

patients with asthma or rheumatoid arthritis, the treatment group was asked to write about the most stressful event in their lives for only twenty minutes over three consecutive days. The control group simply documented daily events. Four months after this singular experience, the lung function of the people in the study group with asthma showed a 20 percent improvement while those in the control group had no change.

The benefit for people with rheumatoid arthritis was even stronger. Those who wrote about stressful events enjoyed a 28 percent reduction in the severity of their disease. Again, the control group showed no improvement.[14] Follow-up studies have confirmed these results. In one study that analyzed the effects of verbal or written emotional expression on rheumatoid arthritis patients, researchers found that three months after their initial journaling or discussion, those who disclosed their feelings walked faster when compared with the control group. And at six months, they had reduced pain and swelling in their joints and less doctor-rated disease activity.[15] Others have found a statistically significant drop in cortisol and interferon gamma (an inflammatory stimulant) in rheumatoid arthritis patients who participate in emotional disclosure.[16]

People with fibromyalgia enjoy similar benefits. A 2005 study tracking the effects of writing about trauma showed improvements in psychological well-being, pain, and fatigue.[17] Other research has demonstrated that at three months, participants who wrote about their emotions had a greater reduction in the overall impact of fibromyalgia, poor sleep, health care utilization, and physical disability than those who were asked to write about time management.[18]

Research has established that psychological stress impairs wound healing by down regulating the immune system.[19] For instance, in a study of fifty-two living kidney donors, it was found that those who had higher preoperative stress and less optimism had delayed wound healing as compared with those who were more emotionally stable.[20] But expressing emotions can mitigate the effects of stress and lead to quicker wound healing by improving immune function. In one British study, for instance, thirty-six participants completed questionnaires measuring emotional distress, loneliness, self-esteem, social support, optimism, and health-related behaviors. The participants then underwent small punch biopsies. One group wrote about traumatic events in their lives while the other wrote about time management. Healing was measured using a high-resolution ultrasound scanner. The first group had significantly smaller wounds fourteen and twenty-one days after the biopsy compared with those in the control.[21]

See Appendix B for web-based resources and patient instructions on how to journal.

Emotional Expression Characterristics Associated with Health

Therapeutic benefit derives from the expression of the emotions themselves. The following key rhetorical characteristics have been most commonly associated with a shift toward improved health.[22]

- The writer constructs an evolving story. People who create a story with a beginning, middle, and end do better than those who repeat the same story day after day. Creating a story transforms the event into one that is easier to understand and learn from.
- The writer develops insight and uses more causal words such as "realize" and "understand."
- The writer develops more optimism, with greater use of positive words and a moderate number of negative words.
- As the story evolves, pronouns changed from first-person singular ("I," "me," "my") to first-person plural ("we," "us," "our"), suggesting that with writing, the person has become less isolated and more connected to his or her community.

I used to tell my patients that they could express these emotions in the privacy of their own homes, that no one need read their writings. I believed that the core therapeutic process was achieved when they provided their stress with an avenue for verbal expression. However, more recent research suggests that I was wrong in this assumption. We now know that the immune system is strengthened when writers are aware that someone will read their journals. It's the sharing that's so important. And that sharing can and should occur verbally as well, to a similar positive effect. People need to know that others are actually listening for these benefits to accrue. This may be another reason why participation in support groups has such a powerfully salutogenic effect on cancer patients.[23]

LISTENING: THE OTHER SIDE OF THE STORY

What's the point of sharing one's deepest thoughts and feelings if the words fall on deaf ears? In one of my favorite classic rock songs, "The Sounds of Silence," Simon and Garfunkel sing of "people hearing without listening." I believe they have identified a human experience that everyone can relate to. The fact is, there are actually two kinds of listening: self-focused (hearing without listening) and other-focused (being available and tuning in). Let's look at these more closely.

Self-Focused Listening

Stephen Covey, author of *The 7 Habits of Highly Successful People*, has written: "Most people do not listen with the intent to understand; they listen with the intent to reply."[24] If the listener is focused on his own thoughts, filtering through past experiences, history, or assumptions as he formulates his response, he will be distracted and inattentive. Indeed, he will actually be multitasking as he mentally accesses personal stories, his own agenda, or potential explanations and advice. This is the best way to carry on a "duologue," not a dialogue.

A patient may be in the midst of expressing some useful ideas or may even be on the verge of an important bit of self-disclosure, but if the caregiver is engaged in self-focused listening, his comment, suggestion, or question will cause the former to stop talking, redirect his attention, and consider what has been interjected.[25] Interruptions are most often self-focused and inhibit speakers from fully voicing their concerns—and they occur all too frequently in the examination room.

Doctors often interfere with their patients' self-disclosure with closed-ended (yes/no) questions. It's their way of controlling the interaction—to the detriment of the people they are charged to serve. Among the many studies examining physician/patient interactions, several have gauged the effect of interruptions. In one study conducted in 1984, fifty-two out of seventy-four patients (69 percent) had exactly eighteen seconds to state their first complaint before their doctor jumped in. In essence, the physicians stopped their patients from sharing more information and blocked the opportunity for them to convey their most pressing fears. Only one of the fifty-two patients who was quickly interrupted got back to his initial concerns and actually finished explaining them to the doctor. Moreover, only 23 percent of the patients listed all of their complaints without the doctor interrupting them. Saving time might have been a motivation for trying to hurry along the interactions, but it usually took only ninety-two seconds for those who made complete statements to get to the end of their list. No one in this study needed more than two and a half minutes for the full disclosure.[26]

Imagine how much more time is lost if the person in need never gets to fully express the issues he's facing. All it takes is a little patience for a meaningful conversation to take place. And in the end, this is more time efficient because the listener obtains the information needed to facilitate positive change rather than provide "word fill" about dull topics that carry little meaning or emotion and detract from a person's well-being.

Moreover, when people have repeated experiences in which they are interrupted and diverted, they become braced for a certain type of unsatisfying interaction, and they alter their own behavior accordingly. Because they feel uncomfortable, they may hold back information they believe is relevant. Or they may phrase it in ways to "win over" the listener—which may not involve saying what they really wanted to say. This is the difference between having a dialogue and being in a debate. Debate means *to beat down*. It's like a sporting event. One side is trying to prove that their arguments are superior to the other's—that their beliefs are more powerful than the other's. This often includes one person projecting his or her point as "the law" even before understanding the other's viewpoint.

Other-Focused Listening

When two people talk, it can take work to reach the topics that matter most. And often that requires adequate time and the right kind of listening. Everyone knows how to listen, but do they know how to listen deeply and with compassion? Other-focused (or deep) listening differs from simple everyday and/or self-focused listening by providing a suffering individual with a presence that allows him to feel safe and undefended. This nurturing environment frees him to express his authentic story.

During such a true dialogue, two people share information that brings forth a deeper understanding. The diversity of thought provides insight to the other that moves one beyond preconceived notions. This is where new discoveries occur in the form of "Aha!" moments. This kind of other-focused listening requires the listener to have a "beginner's mind." She has no agenda and doesn't know (but wants to learn) about what the speaker has to say. She remains quiet as she pays attention to body language, facial expression, and tone of voice. She attunes to the energy and emotions behind the words. Being mindfully present, she also allows for silence, pauses, and space, being aware of details that will allow her to make a more accurate assessment. She takes in as many bits of information as possible in order to absorb as much of the other person's authentic reality as she can. She is truly available to the other person in a way that yogis may be when they say, "Namaste." Literally, this translates into "My soul sees your soul."

If she poses questions, they are in the service of encouraging the conversation to evolve. In that case, they are open-ended queries such as "Tell me more," or "That topic seems to evoke some emotion." A question I have found useful in helping my students and patients understand the dynamic interplay between mind and body is "Where in your body do you carry stress?"

I believe that most caregivers have a lot to learn when it comes to other-focused listening. Doctors dread what has been called the "doorknob moment," when their patients finally blurt out what's really bothering them in the last seconds of the office visit.[27] Often this occurs because the prior discussion has not allowed for the patients to get into their most important issues. Admittedly, many caregivers don't have the luxury of time. But to have a meaningful conversation, trust must be established in a one-on-one interaction without interruptions, allowing the other person's truth to flow sooner rather than later.

Caregivers can learn quite a bit from Thich Nhat Hanh, a Vietnamese Zen Buddhist monk. Along with being a teacher, author, and poet he has been a peace activist since the Vietnam War and was banished from his country at that time because of his pacifism. In the 1960s, Martin Luther King Jr. had nominated him to receive the Nobel Peace Prize. Several years ago, I watched an interview that Oprah Winfrey conducted with this holy man about seeking peace, and although his comments had more to do with quelling anger among warring parties, I believe his statements regarding what he called "deep listening" are compatible with other-focused listening and completely applicable to people who render care to others. The following is an excerpt of this inspiring interview:

Deep listening is the kind of listening that can help relieve the suffering of another person. You can call it compassionate listening. You listen with only one purpose: to help him to empty his heart. Even if he says things that are full of wrong perceptions, full of bitterness, you are still capable of continuing to listen with compassion. Because you know that listening like that, you give that person a chance to suffer less. If you want to help him to correct his perception, you wait for another time. For now, you don't interrupt. You don't argue. If you do, he loses his chance. You just listen with compassion and help him to suffer less. One hour like that can bring transformation and healing.[28]

Unfortunately, when most people wait for their turn to talk, they do not listen like Thich Nhat Hanh, with the purpose to help the others empty their hearts. They have their own agendas. Individuals may listen to only a portion of what is being said because they don't focus their minds on the speaker. It's difficult to listen deeply to someone's feelings when laying out one's next comments or thinking of ways to explain the situation. And the person speaking will surely feel the lack of atunement and clam up.

Some say that learning to listen is more difficult than learning to ask good questions.[29] I believe that is quite true. Hearing what someone says and truly listening to them are two distinct activities. Good listening and observation are the highest forms of emotional intelligence. They precede taking proper action.

THE TRUE VALUE OF LISTENING WELL

When in my rural practice, I had thought that the most powerful drugs in my armamentarium were antidepressants. I would go through the steps of the connection with my patient, and then prescribe the magic . . . fluoxetine 20 mg or sertraline 50 mg. I would ask the patient to return in two weeks, conveying to her the expectation that in fourteen days she should start sleeping better and have more energy. It often worked. But to what do I ascribe the credit? As a society, we give all the power to the pill, when in reality, most of it comes through the caregiver and the therapeutic ritual that occurs even before the pill is prescribed.[30]

Antidepressants and the pharmaceutical companies that sell them have changed cultures. A *New York Times* article documented how Japanese culture, grounded in the Buddhist philosophy that posits there is a reason for suffering (and if people take time to pause and learn from their suffering, they can transcend it), has embraced depression as a disorder. Until 1999, mild to moderate depression was unheard of in Japan— there wasn't even a term for it until Big Pharma introduced *kokoro no kaze*, the notion that "the soul has caught a cold." Since then, the use of antidepressants has soared. The drug companies believed (and rightly so) that depression was being undertreated in Japan. But were more drugs the answer? Once the companies started to market SSRIs heavily and more of them were prescribed, the high suicide rate declined but the culture shifted. Depression is now seen in Japan as something that needs a pill. And today there is greater dependence on a passive treatment than an active, internal exploration to understand and transcend what may be at the root of a person's anguish.

If someone is suffering, there is a *story* to their suffering. Some stories may present themselves as a symptom of pain or depression. This story, when told, can elicit two disparate pro-cesses. One is the habitual, reflexive attachment to a treatment protocol for a symptom. If a patient comes in complaining of heartburn, the clinician turns off the acid with an acid-blocking pill. If, as in Monica's case, blood sugars and blood pressure rise, medications are adjusted accordingly. On the other hand, the caregiver can listen for meaning in the story . . . *What is eating up this person inside? Why is she so stressed out? Why is he eating himself to death?* One approach addresses the physical symptom, the other addresses the deeper meaning beneath the symptom. The first path is linear while the second is circular.

FROM LINEARITY TO CIRCULARITY

Art used to be flat and two-dimensional—consider Egyptian paintings, Greek friezes, and medieval representations of bibli-cal scenes and saints. But then, during the Renaissance, artists discovered how to design a centering point that created three-dimensional perspective—and people came to see the world in a more complex way. Newtonian physics is also linear. Gravity pulls the apple from the tree, and it falls. Today, with the advent of string theory, physics has evolved our understanding of the universe as being subject to multiple realities or perceptions. Indeed, few things in nature are simply linear. Consider the cir-cular patterns of a Fibonacci sequence that occur in the eyes of hurricanes, in conch shells, and in the whorl of seeds around the center of a blooming sunflower. Nature repeats this circular equation multiple times.

Medicine is undergoing a similar transition in thought.

The Fibonacci Sequence

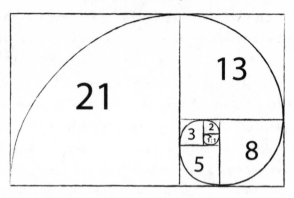

Attaching a drug to a symptom is linear. If a patient has pain that's traced to too much acid in his stomach, the physician will turn off the acid pump with a drug. For the person with heartburn, this linear approach of simply turning off the acid will improve symptoms and help the clinician get on to the next patient, but it can also have negative long-term effects. Chronic acid suppression has been associated with an increased risk of heart disease,[31] kidney disease,[32] and memory loss.[33]

Healing, by contrast, is circular. It is a continuous dialogue between two people that results in a deepening spiral of connection toward meaning that allows caregivers to understand and facilitate self-healing mechanisms. This meaning often results in the release of emotions that motivate patients to move toward salutogenesis. Listening to patients' stories and the context of why they have an upset stomach is much more dynamic than simply turning off the acid pump with a drug. In the final analysis, the healing process requires deep listening, not the habituated reflex of only writing a prescription or ordering a test.

I have had the honor to work with the Veterans Health Administration on a project called Whole Health led by my colleague Tracy Gaudet that is geared toward empowering veterans to be active participants in the health care they receive so it can be organized around what's most important in their lives. The strategy is to use this internal motivation for positive change by integrating the medical care into the context of their lives. We start with different questions, such as "What do you want your health for?" "Where do you feel you need to start to get there?" and "How can we use our expertise in support of your health mission?" I have had the gift of working with many passionate people in the VA health system, one of whom is psychiatrist David Kopacz at the Veterans Administration hospital in Seattle, Washington. He has further delineated the difference between a linear treatment and circular healing.

Linear Treatment	Circular Healing
Pathological process	Natural process
Treatment	Transformation
Restoring old state	Achieving new state
Disease based	Health based
Biomedical model	Health model
Hierarchical	Collaborative
Passive	Active

Caregivers must ask themselves whether they listen to patients in order to fit them into their box of knowledge (as in the linear process) or to help them find their own box (the circular process) that connects them to their deeper meaning. The former gives patients what clinicians know and pulls them into their caregivers' beliefs—the latter explores the patients' connection to themselves, which leads to an authentic healing action. In fact, I believe that this second scenario is where true healing occurs. It requires that patients have the freedom to express an authentic truth that helps them understand how to best move forward. In this process, people always want to get back to the person they were before the illness occurred. But this is never possible because the disorder changes them. If they take time to listen to their own inner thoughts and feelings, they will learn from their illness in a way that can result in a stronger and wiser perspective—and their lives will evolve into a "new normal."

Patients define their own path with the help of someone who cares. Health consumers in this nation are not getting their money's worth because physicians are not listening or

perhaps more accurately, they're not afforded the time to listen for the all-important story that's at the root of the symptom. And when clinicians don't take time to listen, they "cover their asses" by ordering more tests and prescribing more things.[34] These things (frequently, drugs) have side effects and often just suppress a symptom without resolving it. But if they take the time to deeply listen, the cause of the symptom often comes forward, as it did for my patient Monica, and the solution may not be far behind.[35]

ESTABLISHING TRUST WITH MINDFUL LISTENING

The old adage, "We have two ears and one mouth and we should use them proportionally," is so true. Of all the communication skills essential to rapport, the ability to listen well is probably the most important. The best questions in the world will be useless and the information that caregivers glean will be of limited value if they don't know how to listen deeply to the answers. On the other hand, as I explained in Chapter 8, caregivers need to listen with their eyes as well as their ears.

As caregivers listen, along with helping others to unburden their heavy hearts, their goal is to gain insight into their patients' needs and issues. They let their patients know with nonverbal cues that they're available by positioning themselves in a state of readiness: eyes soft and face open, torso slightly bent forward as they make eye contact. (Conversely, cues indicating disinterest can interfere with the other person's willingness to talk if caregivers avert their eyes, read or write notes, attend to their smartphone, or appear bored.) It is important not to "act" but rather to *be* mindful about the task of listening.

The words "medicine" and "meditate" come from the same root—*med*—which means a thoughtful or knowledgeable act to create order. In a mindful, meditative listening state, caregivers can be hyperaware and tuned in to what's happening in the present. They're dropping in, listening with compassion, with their whole heart. They're receiving the information they need to help their patient reach his higher purpose and goals, a state that will facilitate the healing effect. They act thoughtfully to create order.

The key is to let go of any preconceived agenda . . . there's no need to say anything—or to answer feelings with facts. If caregivers sit openly and allow the people they want to help to feel comfortable, they will speak their truths. The caregiver's deep presence gives patients permission to reveal their innermost thoughts and express their meaning.

One of the mysteries of nature is that the closer one gets to something real and authentic, the more beautiful it becomes. The more carefully we examine a flower, a piece of granite, or a cell, a new beauty is revealed with each higher magnification. In deep listening, caregivers uncover another mystery. If what they are listening to is real, beauty starts to unfold . . . the beauty of authentic truth. This is hard to define, but people feel it when it happens. However, that beauty may be illusive unless they turn toward their patients' suffering.

Those who hold on to painful memories try to distract themselves. This is a normal and useful defense mechanism. But it's not until they stop and listen to their own story that they see the authentic cause or need for healing. As caregivers listen to their patients' suffering, they are witnesses to the emptying of their hearts. Indeed, listening to another person's pain requires courage and a willingness to be present with it. This means that caregivers remain undeterred by their own discomfort, fear, anger, or frustration in the face of another's suffering.

THE WISDOM OF SILENCE

Sometimes, it's better to say nothing. The French war hero and president General Charles de Gaulle acted as if silence was the ultimate power tool. He controlled his audiences by looking at them, maintaining eye contact, and keeping his mouth shut. Courtroom lawyers depend on silence when cross-examining witnesses. Often their taciturnity provokes people on the stand to surrender more information or details than they'd planned to. After having asked a question and received the answer, attorneys will stop talking as a way to indicate that the witness must have more to say. And often he or she falls for this ploy and spills some of the beans.

But silence can also have therapeutic benefits, especially when giving a person room to unburden. In *What to Do When Someone You Love Is Depressed*, psychologist Mitch Golant wrote about the value of silence when someone is hurting. "Your role in these moments," he explained, "is to be a beacon of light, flashing the proximity of the shore without comment. The beacon does no harm. It simply says, 'I'm here; I'm listening; I care.' It offers a semblance of connection, showing the way toward safety."[36] Indeed, not only does the beacon do no harm,

I believe that it does a lot of good when the person who is hurting knows someone is there and cares.

There is much to be said about the wisdom and even the pain of silence, but caregivers don't always heed this maxim. When interactions between physicians and patients are analyzed, it becomes obvious that doctors do most of the talking. However, when asked, physicians usually think the reverse is true.[37] It's a subtle dance. The less the physician talks, the more the patient will say, as if to fill the void. In fact, a caregiver's silence can be as effective as direct questions to draw out meaningful information.

Caregivers must watch their timing, though. They can remain silent if they're fairly certain the patient has more to say, and their silence is useful if he is more inclined to fill the gap than they are. He can indicate this nonverbally by steepling his hands or using the other gestures outlined in the previous chapter. If the silence is coupled with caregivers shifting in the chair or nodding and smiling as if to say, "Go on . . ." they can be more effective in eliciting information than if they actually say those words. In fact, verbalizing encouraging statements such as "Go on," can be distracting, and may interfere with an individual's willingness to share more.

There are different kinds of silence. The easy quiet between intimate partners or family members is special to witness, as a room can fill with love and compassion without the jumble of words to interfere. However, in our small-group discussions with medical students in The Healer's Art course, there can be rather long periods of silence. This generally makes the medical students (and the faculty leaders) squirm. But that's a method of teaching. . . . *Why do people feel uncomfortable in silence? Why do they feel they need to fill the void with words?*

DEEP LISTENING AND CULTURAL COMPETENCY

Much has been written about developing caregivers' cultural competency because the most effective interventions occur when we match the best evidence-based therapies to patients' beliefs and culture. That is the goal. But so many cultures exist in the world—no one can truly be expert in every one of them. There are even many subcultures within our own society that may feel foreign to individuals such as those of people who have been raised in different parts of the country, those who belong to the LGBTQ community, those whose religious beliefs and practices differ, and those of immigrants or other minorities. Everyone wants to be culturally competent and to respect all the people with whom they come into contact, without knowing every politically correct fact so as not to offend. This is a difficult task at best.

However, I feel that deep listening helps caregivers jump the barriers that cultures may artificially erect in front of them. When caregivers practice it, they can get a read on individuals' true inner selves that honors their culture because they are connecting human to human. When they pause, get out of their heads, and listen compassionately, they make strides toward seeing life through the patients' unique lenses. They become culturally competent because they resonate with others beneath their skin color, history and heritage, and the behaviors that might evoke anxiety or judgments, beneath what I like to think of as their cultural overcoats.

To appreciate what others need, caregivers must first become aware of how they see the world so they are careful not to project what they "know" upon others too quickly. Only by self-awareness and compassionate, deep listening will they be able to transpose their own perceptions toward an understanding of how patients see their world. Then caregivers will be able to recruit their expertise in service of the greater good. And together with their patients, they can then develop action toward health.

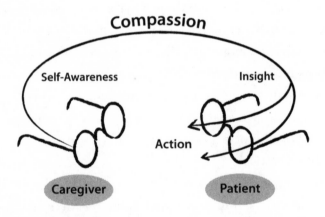

I recently had the experience of connecting with a couple that had just moved to Wisconsin from Saudi Arabia. They had been in the States for only five weeks, and the wife was about to deliver their second child. Her husband spoke English, but she did not. Knowing how people from that region of the world value a woman's honor and privacy, I had some trepidation about attending this birth. But my initial fears were ill founded.

When I have the opportunity to deliver a baby, it's a great moment for me to practice mindful presence. This time, the baby came quickly and emerged with a single big push. The cord was wrapped around his neck. We slipped it off and placed the infant on his mother's chest. She immediately broke into loud chanting in Arabic. I understood the intent but not the words; she was offering a prayer for her newborn. The father began crying, and the nurse and I paused. We all connected, feeling the couple's joy and the realization that this was a beautiful moment we could share. Despite the language and cultural issues, I knew this woman appreciated that I was fully available to her. In fact, just then, culture didn't really matter to any of us. I cut the cord and let this mother breast-feed her newborn son—a look of rapture slowly spreading on her face as she gazed into his eyes.

This birth reminded me again that there is much more to all of us than we realize. We all can become "culturally competent" by simply connecting to that other human being in a deep, compassionate, and respectful way.

10

Move from Burnout toward Beauty

It Felt Love

How
Did the rose
Ever open its heart

And give this world
All its
Beauty?

It felt the encouragement of light
Against its
Being,

Otherwise,
We all remain

Too

Frightened.

—HAFIZ, from "The Gift," Daniel Ladinsky, translator[1]

On many occasions, my patients come to their medical visits with family caregivers. The latter are often responsible for the physical and emotional well-being of their ailing relatives—and it can be an exhausting job. Although not the identified patients, I look for ways to engage the caregivers so that they can carry on in better spirits. Linda always accompanied her ninety-year-old mother, Millie, to my office. Millie was suffering from a wide array of age-related conditions: cardiovascular disease and congestive heart failure, a leaky aortic valve, high cholesterol and blood pressure, a minor stroke, osteoporosis, diabetes, severe neuropathy in her feet (a side effect of the diabetes), and a form of vascular dementia that didn't leave her as forgetful as Alzheimer's would. In fact, Millie remembered all the struggles in her life in exquisite detail, and couldn't stop reciting them tearfully to herself and everyone else who came in contact with her in an endless litany of suffering.

Millie had been a vivacious, intelligent, and beautiful woman well into her mideighties, so Linda was grief stricken about what had become of her over the last few years. As Millie's condition worsened, Linda became increasingly haggard and distressed. Even though she wasn't my "patient," I felt she needed at least as much attention as Millie did. Spiritual writer L. Thomas Holdcroft has written, "Life is a grindstone. Whether it grinds us down or polishes us up, depends on us." I could see the toll Millie's care was taking on Linda. It was clear to me that she was on the verge of burnout.

Caregiver burnout, especially among family members, has potentially catastrophic and widespread consequences in the United States. Only a tiny fraction (4–5 percent) of people needing care receive it in institutions such as nursing homes.[2] Consequently, most people turn to family and friends for help. In fact, the proportion of adult children providing personal care and/or financial assistance to a parent has more than tripled since the late 1990s. Currently, 25 percent of adult children, mostly Baby Boomers, provide care for their parents.[3] In 2009, AARP's Public Policy Institute estimated that more than sixty-one million households in the United States had family caregivers in place.[4] Given the aging of our population, that number will continue to grow.

Family caregiving can also have severe financial repercussions that can create additional psychosocial problems. Many people adopting the role must quit their jobs or turn to part-time work because of their responsibilities. In 2011, MetLife Insurance Company published a study showing how devastating lifetime income loss can be due to family caregiving responsibilities: total wage, Social Security, and private pension losses over a lifetime due to caregiving could typically range from $283,716 for men to $324,044 for women, or $303,880 on average. When this amount is multiplied by the 9.7 million people age fifty or more who are caring for a loved one, the amount totals nearly $3 trillion. Financial hardships may be stressful enough, but staying on the job while maintaining the caregiver role is equally difficult. The MetLife study also reported that adult children over the age of fifty who continue to work while providing care to their parents are more likely to have only fair or poor health outcomes themselves when compared with those who are not caregivers.[5]

Burnout is widespread not only among family caregivers—

clinicians can suffer from it, too. In fact, a Mayo Clinic survey of 35,922 physicians showed an increase in burnout symptoms from 45 percent in 2011 to 54.4 percent in 2014. That means more than half of all physicians were found to be experiencing symptoms of professional burnout.[6] This can create profound repercussions. Often, the first thing to go when doctors reach this state is *not* the ability to prescribe a drug or perform a surgical procedure. Rather, it's compassion, the ability to listen, and patience—the most important ingredients clinicians need to form a healing connection.[7] One of the earliest symptoms of burnout among doctors is depersonalization. That's when they see their patients as objects or diagnostic codes rather than human beings with life stories to share. What's worse, research has shown that the more emotional exhaustion medical students experience, the more likely they are to cheat or perform dishonest acts.[8]

How do caregivers preserve a sense of balance—neither withholding attention nor giving beyond their limits? It is possible. In fact, not only can caregivers maintain wholeness, they can even find joy, meaning, and wisdom in their role. But first, they must recognize and deal with burnout.

THE SOURCES OF BURNOUT

Neuroimaging studies have shown that the same networks in the brain are activated whether people receive a painful stimulus themselves or are merely witnessing someone else receiving the stimulus—the mirror neurons at work again.[9] Empathy consists of this capacity to recognize another person's emotions and share in them. Indeed, empathy *training* activates centers of the brain (the anterior insula and midcingulate cortex) associated with pain and negative mood.[10] Caregivers feel *with* the other person. (The word comes from the Greek *empatheia*, or "suffering with," and is influenced by the German *Einfuhlung*, which means "feeling into.") So they experience joy when a loved one is happy, sadness when she is unhappy, and pain when she is suffering.

Although empathy is crucial for successful social interactions (people lacking empathy are said to be sociopaths), researchers have found that disproportionate sharing of others' negative emotions may be maladaptive and can constitute a source of burnout.[11] An empathic person literally feels the pain of the other. "If you hurt, I hurt." This can lead to empathic distress, a state in which caregivers cannot distinguish their own feelings from another's—and share the anguish to excess. It is contagious and flows from one person to the next, especially if helpers feel they need to fix another's suffering. But that's a setup for failure because suffering cannot be "fixed."

Unfortunately, empathic distress can evolve into an aversion to the person or situation. To protect themselves, caregivers withdraw, or if they're unable to retreat, they can feel trapped and become resentful. And so they experience burnout: the sense of being totally overwhelmed and burdened without any hope of reward or change. This matches the classic definition of stress, which is the perception that one cannot meet the demands of one's environment.[12]

A similar breakdown among doctors and other professionals usually arises when they're asked to see more patients in a day than they can possibly manage well. They cram peoples' lives into fifteen-minute-or-less office visits that leave them little time to create a meaningful connection. In this unsatisfying process, they never get at the root of their patients' problems. They don't know what their patients really need and consequently feel guilty and inadequate. They lose the ability to connect.

I am not immune to burnout myself and will withdraw if I'm drained. In my practice, it is essential for me to sense my patients' stories. This mutual feeling enhances our connection and gives both of us insight into information we'll need for healing. But when I am exhausted, this skill is the first to evaporate. I don't *feel* my patients, and they turn into a list of complaints to which I attach a disease label and for which I prescribe a drug. We can all feel the expanding distance. Consequently, they suppress parts of their story, I am less effective, and the recovery we're seeking eludes us.

Professional burnout can also occur when clinicians encounter a person who resists their help by constantly offering excuses or getting angry if they dare suggest changes. This can be frustrating, so I find it more therapeutic to reframe the patient's defensive behavior as part of a healing process. I tell my medical students, "Never work harder than your patients." Caregivers may step back from helping these challenging individuals, but they need not give up on them. One strategy is to recognize that they may be in what has sometimes been called the "precontemplative state." Students are taught to recognize that these patients are still in an early stage of the healing process—perhaps in denial—and aren't yet ready to reflect on their true situation or consider taking action. In this case, doctors can guide the steps of change by encouraging self-reflection, without pushing patients too much or too early.

THE CONSEQUENCES OF BURNOUT

Family caregivers often devote eighteen hours a day or more to their loved one—far more than they would have spent working at a job. They can be on call around the clock, without opportunities for vacations or respite. This puts them at great risk for burnout. People can't assist suffering individuals if they are suffering themselves, so burnout is a dangerous state for both. Common physical and emotional signs include headaches, backaches, insomnia, and gastrointestinal disturbances; physical and mental exhaustion; rashes; persistent colds; heart palpitations and chest pain; frustration, irritability, and anger; sadness and hopelessness; difficulties concentrating; resentment; low self-esteem; and depression.[13]

I believe that the potential for burnout is unique for each caregiver. However, from my experience, it looms particularly ominously if people don't maintain their own personal equilibrium; keep good social connections; recharge; and reconnect with what gives their lives meaning, value, and purpose. There is no right balance—only what works best for each individual—but there are ways to seek and attain it.

FINDING BALANCE AND GOOD HEALTH
IN COMPASSION

It's important to note that in addition to empathic distress, feelings of empathy can give rise to a second, more positive emotion: compassion ("co-passion"). This is a sense of warmth and concern toward the person who is hurting that's coupled with a strong desire to improve his outcome. Visualize a young child in the hospital with an upset and anxious mother. She can hardly bear to be near her sick son. Instead, she avoids intimate contact with him, pacing back and forth in the hall as she awaits word from the doctor.[14] Now imagine that same child, but this time his mother sits at his bedside, holding his hand and comforting him with her gentle, loving words. It's easy to see which scenario is more soothing and helpful to the child—which conveys empathic distress and which conveys compassion.

Compassion is the antidote to empathic distress. It implies, *I may not be able to fix your suffering, but I can simply be with you as we both turn toward its cause and walk to a better place together.* This is the feeling of interconnection in which two individuals are joined in the same process, and it is an effective helping strategy. Indeed, research shows that individuals who feel and express compassion are able to give more than those who rely on empathy alone.[15]

The good news is that scientists have now also proven that being compassionate not only helps the person in need but also benefits the caregiver emotionally as well as physically.[16] The positive emotions that arise from feeling compassion elevate immune function as compared with anger, which depresses it. These feelings engage the neuroplasticity of the brain by activating the prefrontal cortex and ventral striatum, regions that are also stimulated by social connection, maternal affiliation, and romantic love. This brain activity helps reverse the negative emotions associated with burnout, thus strengthening resilience.[17]

Indeed, recently, researchers at the University of Buffalo showed that caring for others enhances a caregiver's health. The act of volunteering protects people from stressful events in their lives, and this in turn has a positive effect on the long-term survival rates and the distress levels of the volunteers. Interestingly, this stress-buffering effect worked only for individuals who had positive views of others and were not cynical.[18] I believe that oxytocin plays a role in the longevity of these volunteers. It increases when people connect and drives them to build social relationships while reducing inflammation and protecting the heart.

Another fascinating study published in 2014 explored the potentially beneficial effects within the brains of people who give support to loved ones. In this experiment, twenty romantically attached couples completed an fMRI session in which the female partner underwent a scan while her partner stood just outside the scanner and received unpleasant electric shocks. The women were provided with one of two coping mechanisms. Either they were to squeeze a stress ball when the shocks were administered to their loved one, or they held his hand and thought about sending love and support. The stress ball did not change the women's brains at all. But in those women who offered caring and intention, the reward-related region called the ventral striatum, the same area activated by compassion and maternal behavior, lit up. There was also less activity in the amygdala, the structure that responds to fear.[19]

This is a great example of how opening and engaging the source of suffering can create a biology that builds courage, hope, and resilience, establishing a catalyst for the connection. Offering love and support can also be a form of self-care—as people turn the same intent upon themselves. These studies teach us that compassion produces intention for others, and in so doing, it's also the best way to reduce one's own stress.

Other researchers looked at how compassion enhances health by comparing immune reactions of three groups of subjects. The first group generated caring and compassionate emotions by one of two methods: watching a video of Mother Teresa ministering to the sick and dying or shifting their attention to the area around their hearts (where most people experience positive emotions) and meditating on loving and compassionate emotions within themselves. The second group generated angry and frustrating thoughts either by recalling difficult incidents from their own lives or watching specially edited, disturbing clips of war scenes. A third group acted as controls. The researchers found that those who meditated on compassionate emotions produced a significantly stronger and longer immune response (as measured by an infection-fighting antibody in their saliva called IgA) than the study participants who focused on anger and frustration or who did no visualizations at all.[20]

Curing is linear and goes in one direction from the caregiver to the patient. But, as we've seen, a healing connection is circular. In the process of healing another, people also heal themselves. When individuals reach out with compassion, they're not serving someone other than themselves—they're serving one *interconnected* process that includes themselves. It becomes increasingly clear that in order to help others, caregivers must first start with being compassionate toward themselves.

I believe that the best way to do this is to engage in compassionate mindfulness meditation. This activity derives from Buddhist contemplative practices. It reinforces inner calmness, a strong mind, and the courageous determination to help someone who is suffering.[21] Fortunately, it can be learned and is a valuable part of a caregiver's armamentarium. Engaging in this meditation is also associated with many health benefits for the caregiver including a reduction in inflammation. This lessens the risk of many chronic diseases[22]—such as diabetes,[23] cancer, and Alzheimer's—that are dependent on inflammation for their progression. Research has established that people who practice compassionate mindfulness meditation have down regulated the genes that promote inflammation with less interleukin-6 (a marker of inflammation) circulating in their blood.[24]

Another excellent avenue to expand compassion is the loving-kindness meditation, which is found in Appendix A. This exercise evokes compassion, kindness, and acceptance toward oneself and others. Practitioners send out feelings of loving kindness in expanding circles first for themselves and then to people near and far. Research comparing empathy to compassion showed that people experience more positive affect with compassion training.[25] During this meditation, individuals activate regions of the brain that light up with love and pleasure and produce more oxytocin. As they feel and express love, they experience less burnout. It is hard to be irritable and impatient when one is connected to oneself and others in this loving way.

MINDFULNESS ALSO FOSTERS CREATIVITY IN CAREGIVING

Pausing and being mindful may help create space that invites creative thought. New ideas come from the process of people getting out of their habituated neuro-networks, which allows for new neuro-networks to form and become reinforced. In fact, international research has shown that openness during mindful meditation can lead to creative insights. In one investigation, conducted by psychologist Lorenza Colzato at the University of Leiden, subjects were asked to practice two types of meditation: one group focused on a part of their bodies during inhalations and exhalations, and the other meditated on statements such as "I'm open," "I let go," "I expand my consciousness," and "I accept myself as I am." The latter is related to mindfulness because when emotions arose, the practitioners observed them without judgments.

Next, all of the participants were given two tasks. One involved convergent thinking. They were provided three words ("time," "hair," and "stretch") and asked what they had in common. They had to collapse three concepts into one idea. (By the way, the answer is "long.") This is the type of concrete thinking needed to find an answer. Then they were given a task that highlighted divergent thinking. They had to list as many possible and unusual uses as they could for six common items: brick, towel, shoe, newspaper, pen, and bottle. Divergent thinking requires creativity. It turned out that the people who practiced the more open meditations were quicker on the divergent tasks than were the more focused meditators.[26]

The outcome of this research has two lessons for caregivers. First, when individuals don't attach themselves to any one belief, they're open to creativity. Openness allows them to develop new insights into their patients' reality. The "letting go" meditation practice breaks people out of their critical, analytical, convergent thinking—their habituated neuro-networks of comfort—which can get them stuck in old biases laid down in the brain years ago. Through the miracle of brain plasticity, creativity helps caregivers build new synapses that allow them to appreciate patients' lives in novel ways. When they leave behind the conditioned mind and projected beliefs and start seeing others as they truly are, they move toward the more authentic reality of beauty. So, when sitting with patients, caregivers do focus on them, but they should do that with an openness to whatever comes, without judgment. People suffer. Caregivers shouldn't judge their suffering, but be brave enough to turn toward it in an open and accepting way.

The second lesson is that mindfulness meditation enhanced the participants' ability to be creative and make mental leaps. These sudden flashes of insight provide a sense of awe. Perhaps not surprisingly, that feeling has health benefits, too. A stagnant, stuck brain is an unhealthy brain. The same is true for the body. It is much better to experience "Aha!" moments that allow people to appreciate the mystery and beauty in life. These sudden perceptions are also how neuro-networks form in the brain. It's what creates the pathways that are needed for neuro-plasticity to occur. I think of it as an established highway (old brain) now branching off into new roads that allow the person to experience images of beauty. This is what connects us to awe . . . the vision of something novel and inspiring. Johann Sebastian Bach, the famous musical composer, resonated with this when he was asked about how he was able to create such beautiful melodies. "The problem is not finding [melodies], it's—when getting up in the morning and out of bed—not stepping on them."[27]

For me, seeing the human potential to heal is always an "awesome" moment. But caregivers won't entertain that possibility if they're too busy judging and analyzing without taking the time to engage in and appreciate the connection. Both are vital but need to be put into an order that is most efficient. Open first, then use that information to plan a strategy toward health.

When reaching out with compassion to an ailing friend or loved one or even to a patient or client or coworker, the connection can restore one's sense of purpose as a helper, healer, and supporter. Ultimately, as two people connect, both experience the power of their own potential, gain greater appreciation for each other's truths, heal each other, and find a sense of beauty.

MOVING TOWARD BEAUTY WITH A "SPIRITUAL ANCHOR"

A "spiritual anchor" is an object that reminds people of what gives their lives meaning and purpose and consequently why they may want to change their behavior. It's a talisman that connects to the most powerful neuro-networks in the central nervous system—those that influence behaviors. This is because meaning and purpose are strongly related to emotions that "emote movement" toward healthy choices—choices people make because they are associated with what matters most to them.

My spiritual anchor is a small stone. Sometimes I keep it on my desk, but most of the time, it resides in my pocket. Why is this stone so important to me? Many years ago, my family and I were at a beach that was covered with lots of little stones. My youngest child seemed to be staring at a pile of them for no less than twenty minutes. Finally, he came over to where I was sitting and presented me with a black one. It was round and smooth and earthy. "Dad, I found this for you," he said proudly. My heart soared. This was so beautiful. My son was searching for the perfect stone for his father. His act of love touched me deeply.

When I'm having a bad day, or I don't get a grant I've been working on for months, or I have an argument with my wife, I will stick my hand in my pocket and connect with what gives meaning and purpose to my life. It's a reminder for me of why I want to move ahead, to be a good person, to spread positive energy. Even in the bleakest of times, it helps me recall the goodness of our lives. That's what spirituality is—a connection that gives our lives meaning and purpose. (The range can be broad here: watching one's children grow and marry, living to see one's grandchildren, traveling, making significant contributions at work, and so on.) Sadly, due to our constant busyness, we often need reminders that bring us back to the basics. For me, it's this small stone.

I use this tool in the clinical setting with my patients all the time. I ask them to share with me what they consider their spiritual anchor. We talk about it and use it to help them keep on track for healing and recovery. One patient, Jeff, went through the difficult work of renouncing alcohol. When I asked him how he accomplished this, he told me, "I wanted to be a gardener and to cultivate a healthy soil for my children to grow and flourish in." He knew that his drinking was setting a bad example for them, and that motivated him to stop.

But soon, as happens so often with alcoholics in remission, Jeff became addicted to something else. In his case, it was food. His uncontrolled eating led to obesity coupled with diabetes. So I said to him, "It looks as if food is making you unhealthy the same way that the alcohol did. Two weeks from now, I'd like you to bring to my office a physical object that reminds you of why you would want to watch what you eat and why you want to lose weight. I want you to be able to keep this on your body so you can connect to it when you need to, especially before you open the refrigerator."

Two weeks passed, and Jeff presented himself in my office empty-handed. So I asked him, "Did you find a spiritual anchor and bring it with you today?" Silently, but with a twinkle in his eye, he lifted his right trouser leg and pulled down his sock. On the inside of his lower leg was a new tattoo of a gardener hoeing a garden. "If I want a dessert," he told me triumphantly, "I look at my tattoo. It reminds me of my children and their welfare. It's going to help me lose weight." Today, Jeff still has diabetes, but he has it under much better control because he has successfully slimmed down!

Whenever people have a sense of control, it provides focus and allows them to have confidence and the belief that they can overcome their current adversity. For the caregiver's part, this means concentrating on and structuring the chaos, fear, and uncertainty and then turning it into pragmatic steps that patients can take to overcome their suffering, anxiety, and illness. A spiritual anchor can be a useful tool in this process. To be sure, knowing what people want their health for is essential. It's the fulcrum of change. Awareness of its significance stimulates emotions that motivate new, more healthful behaviors. Caregivers need to know what really matters to the person they want to help or she won't change. And they have to help her understand for herself why she would be better off conducting her life differently.

When caregivers encourage this kind of self-reflection, it helps their patients or those they love appreciate the discordance between what they're doing and what they really want in life. The recognition of this disconnect helps them stop a detrimental behavior. They ask the person who loves to eat, "What do you like about your current lifestyle? Do you want to be around to continue enjoying great meals with your friends and family?" Once they realize how their behavior conflicts with their life's meaning, they often decide to change on their own.

The spiritual anchor is a symbol of why people want to live better lives. But it has to come from within each individual. Caregivers can encourage others to find theirs. I've got my stone.

FINDING BEAUTY IN SUFFERING

At 2 a.m. one morning while I was still working in Driggs, Idaho, I was awakened by an emergency call from a nurse at our small hospital. She summoned me to the ER to see a patient who was complaining of devastating headaches. Somewhat begrudgingly, I dragged myself out of bed and headed to the hospital. When I walked into the ER, I saw Becky curled up in a fetal position on the gurney, rocking back and forth. Pale, with disheveled blond hair and trembling hands, I could see that she was really suffering. My initial perception was that she was a "chronic pain patient." Believe me, part of me was thinking, *How do I get her out of the ER as fast as possible so I can go back to bed?* I am only human, after all. But as a small-town doc, I also wanted to do all I could to help her. If I didn't, who would? So I needed to get at the root of Becky's problem. I sat down to talk to her.

There, in the wee hours of the morning, this young woman shared with me a history of shocking abuse. I took great interest in her situation and continued to explore her issues with her during follow-up appointments. Soon we became good friends. Becky experienced fewer headaches after these compassionate talks—for which she was quite grateful and so was I. And when I got set to leave Driggs, she gave me a meditation robin made of blue glass as a memento of our friendship. I keep it on my desk as a constant reminder of how beauty can shine through suffering.

Had I perceived Becky as merely a "chronic pain patient"— sending her on her way with a shot of pain meds but without our having had the chance to talk deeply—I wouldn't have been any better off, and she certainly wouldn't have been any better off. But her struggle had great meaning for me, and now I also had a lovely spiritual anchor to remind me of her and the good that comes when approaching caregiving tasks with a loving and open heart. At times like these, I feel that I should pay my patients instead of them paying me.

From my work since then, I have often found beauty to emerge from the profoundest despair. This is true not only in medicine. Glorious music, literature, and art have come out of suffering. Singer-songwriter Tracy Chapman grew up in an abusive, poor, and challenging environment, yet out of those difficult times she wrote deeply meaningful music. J. K. Rowling, the author of the wildly beloved *Harry Potter* books, was homeless and lived in her car with her daughter for a while. Going back in history, Vincent van Gogh is an obvious exemplar as are Edgar Allan Poe and Beethoven (who wrote some of his most admired works while totally deaf). So much beauty can be forged in difficult situations.

Yet some people believe that caregiving is a draining enterprise. That it can leave one mentally and physically exhausted and is best relegated to others with more "saintly" or self-sacrificing temperaments. I have found the opposite to be true. Rather than sapping me, when I engage all of the elements of the compassionate connection, the caregiving process not only energizes me but also enhances my health and lifts my spirits.

Psychologist Dr. Mitch Golant has spent years conducting research for the Cancer Support Community on the benefits of psychosocial support for cancer patients and their families. Before he began this phase of his career, he led the very support groups that he later began to study. In fact, by his count, he has facilitated nearly fifteen thousand groups. He told me that whenever he explained to people what he did, their faces fell.

"That must be so depressing," they would say to him, mournfully. "I can't imagine doing that kind of work. It must be so difficult." He could almost feel them backing away.

"On the contrary," Mitch would say. "It's the most uplifting work you can imagine. People are so motivated to make positive changes in their lives. Their strength and resilience as they join their medical team in their fight for recovery is totally inspiring. It's the most exciting work I've ever done."

One can approach caregiving as an exhausting experience that leads to withdrawal and depression, or like Mitch Golant, the same process can be perceived in a new, more optimistic way with love and compassion. Some would say that individuals are born with a certain attitude toward life, but I think everyone is trainable. This reminds me of a parable that Rachel Naomi Remen tells of three stone masons building a cathedral in the fourteenth century. Briefly, it goes something like this:

A monk who was supervising the work wanted to assess the attitudes of his workers so he approached three masons cutting large stones for the cathedral. The monk asked of the first mason, "Tell me about your job."

"It's awful," he replied. "I break my back and work these long hours, for what? I'll never see this cathedral finished. I don't get paid very much. My boss is a jerk. I wish I could do something else."

The monk went on to the second mason and asked him the same question. "Oh, it's not so bad," he said. "I make enough to put food on the table, a roof over our heads, and clothes on my kids' backs. I've been able to pay for their schooling, so they'll have a better life than me."

The third mason had a different response altogether. "What a privilege it is to build this beautiful church. I get to practice my skills in the service of others. And centuries from now, people will still come here from all over the country to pray and connect to God," he said with eyes aglow.

This mason had found the beauty in his work.

OPENING

A few years ago, I participated in a five-day *silent* retreat with Jon Kabat-Zinn in the Catskills—a mountainous, wooded setting in upstate New York. Kabat-Zinn is one of the modern founders of the mindfulness meditation movement, and I was eager to attend because I wanted to pick his brain and absorb his knowledge. I'd hoped that he would impart to me his many pearls of wisdom.

I arrived, unpacked, and joined the group. After initial introductions, we laid on the floor and did a body scan, during which many of us fell asleep. The synchronized snoring prompted giggles around the room. We were an exhausted group of hard workers, after all. Then Kabat-Zinn asked us to grab a cushion for a sitting meditation without speaking to anyone. That lasted for about an hour. After that, we stood and did a silent walking meditation, during which we paid very close attention to each step we took without looking at anyone else. It was a really slow thirty minutes. Then we did another sitting meditation. And another walking one. This went on morning, noon, and night with silent breaks for meals. Some teachings were interspersed but not many.

In their everyday lives, people get used to constant activity, interaction, and thought. But when their minds are busy, and they're told to be silent, they can experience withdrawal from the chaos of life. So, day 2 dawned with me feeling frustrated. I wasn't getting what I'd come for. I wasn't downloading enough information. I wanted to do a mind-meld with my mentor, but he wasn't talking all that much! Even though it was maddening, I continued on through days 2, 3, and 4 with no change in routine. Just sitting, walking, eating, repeat. Sitting, walking, eating, repeat.

Then at 10 p.m. on day 4, it happened. During the walking meditation, I felt a gentle breeze through the aspens. The leaves tinkled like crystals on a chandelier. The full moon illuminated our surroundings. Suddenly, everything came alive—like in a scene from the movie *Avatar*. The forest pulsated with life. I felt hyperaware of the environment. I had gotten out of my head. It was so touching and beautiful. The radiant moon, the leaves on the trees, the rhythm of the forest were all palpable.

Then, as we prepared to go home on day 5, our silence ended. And after not making eye contact or talking for three or four days, we were asked to do just that. I sat in front of a Midwestern businessman, and we looked each other in the eye. Both of us started crying. We weren't sad. After getting out of the clutter of the mind, we saw the beauty; we could feel it. There we were, just two guys looking at each other and weeping. But when we started to talk, the beauty began drifting away. Once we got into our heads, we wanted to tell each other what we'd learned. Now, there was pressure. And slowly we reenculturated into our lives.

I sit with people as they die. Many of them have never seen that beauty until they're on their deathbeds. Some seem to glow before the end. They forgive their childhoods. They turn toward what was most important in their lives. And they are grateful for those transcendent moments.

Most caregivers don't go to those places that matter most unless they are brave enough to turn toward suffering. In my career, I have heard many accounts of abuse, trauma, alcoholism, drug use, homelessness, and injustice. The experiences that caused the suffering and harm are not beautiful, but the process of turning toward them and giving them attention helps us find a path that heals. If caregivers open themselves to how those traumas affect a person's life, they can feel that they are touching an authentic truth within. This becomes beautiful when we are able to explore the source of the emotional pain so that healing can occur. Everything suddenly snaps into focus. Life is more vibrant, less "gray." The experience is energizing and joyful. It leads to new insights and creative energy. It points toward meaning where two people are able to find a common road toward a better place. And once both give suffering their attention, they develop the profound connection that gives them the ability to heal and be healed.

The potential to sense beauty such as this is in all of us. We just have to open to it.

Compassion Training

Throughout *The Compassionate Connection,* I have written about how to be mindful in interactions with the people you want to help. On several occasions, I have recommended mindfulness mediations. This is different from simply being "mindful" and aware of what you're doing. Structured exercises such as these ask you to set aside five or ten minutes several times a week to draw on your inner resources for strength and compassion. They can exponentially enhance your ability to connect in a positive way.

Until I started to practice mindfulness meditation, I was unable to fully get my mind out of my own clutter—my biases, my busyness, my distractions. But the repeated act of pausing and focusing the mind that occurs during mindfulness medi-tation allowed my mirror neurons to be more sensitive to oth-ers' feelings. I had never experienced this prior to having a centering practice.

"Practice" is the operant word here. We build biceps at the gym with more curls . . . but we can also build conscious insight—that wonderful moment when two well-established synapses start to cross-communicate in our brain—with mindful compassion training.

In the *Dhammapda*, the sayings of the Buddha, it has been written:

"The thought manifests as the word;

The word manifests as the deed;

The deed develops into habit;

And habit hardens into character;

So watch the thought and its way with care,

And let it spring from love born out of concern

   for all beings. . . ."

. . .

Some practical hints before you begin: Read through the meditation. It's difficult to meditate and read at the same time, so your next step will be to record it, imagining that you're speaking to yourself—because, in fact you will be. Read slowly, stopping between sentences, allowing each word to sink in. I have indicated some natural pauses where you may want to allow a few minutes of silence to go by. Once you've created the recordings, find a comfortable place (either seated or reclining), make sure you won't be interrupted, and close your eyes.

Focus on your breathing. Place one hand on your chest and the other on your abdomen. When you take a deep breath, the hand on your abdomen should expand more than the one on the chest. This ensures that your diaphragm is expanding, pulling air into the base of your lungs. Take a slow deep breath in through your nose, imagining that you are sucking in all the air in the room, and hold it for a count of three or four. Slowly exhale through your mouth for a count of six to eight. The exhalation should be twice as long as the inhalation. Repeat the cycle four more times for a total of five deep breaths. Try to reduce your breathing to six breaths per minute (one breath every ten seconds). This is the optimal rate to stimulate relaxation of the autonomic nervous system.

THE LOVING-KINDNESS MINDFULNESS MEDITATION

The loving-kindness meditation comes from Buddhist philosophy. This twenty-five-hundred-year-old practice creates and reinforces the consciousness that a web of interconnectedness exists among all people. The bond to everyone in the world is also spiritual and emotional. Rachel Naomi Remen has written, "When we know ourselves to be connected to all others, acting compassionately is simply the natural thing to do." The realization that you are part of an interconnected universe helps you understand that if you are not well, I am not well; and if I am not well, you are not well. The loving-kindness meditation can be used to reinforce unconditional love and open the heart toward others and oneself. It is another way in which people can grow and find joy when they step into a caregiving role.

The UCLA Mindfulness Awareness Research Center

(MARC) has a free version of the loving-kindness meditation that can be listened to online: http://marc.ucla.edu/mpeg/05_Loving_Kindness_Meditation.mp3. The University of Wisconsin also has a number of guided meditations on their website that can be logged into and followed: http://www.fammed.wisc.edu/our-department/media/968/guided-loving-kindness. Readers who wish to create their own practice can just follow the directions below. They are adapted from the University of Wisconsin model.

Before beginning, please follow the breathing and recording suggestions made above.

The Loving-Kindness Mindfulness Meditation

[BEGIN AUDIOTAPING HERE.]

The loving-kindness meditation evokes compassion, kindness, and acceptance toward ourselves and others. It will reconnect you to the heart of tenderness inside you. It's like meeting a wise being who understands your life and holds it dear. Even in the greatest of suffering, it is possible for the heart to hold it all.

Release any tightness in your body—your belly, arms, shoulders, face, jaw.

Now sense the part of your body in which you feel compassion, kindness, and caring—it could be the area around your heart. Allow that area to soften with each breath. Notice any thoughts that may arise as you hold this area in your awareness.

Ask yourself: What do I wish for most in my life? *Which phrases . . .*

- *May I be safe and protected.*
- *May I be peaceful and at ease.*
- *May I feel joy.*
- *May I be well and strong.*
- *May I be free of fear and anxiety.*
- *May I be filled with loving kindness.*
- *May I accept myself as I am.*

Now imagine someone you know who is easy to love and care about. It could be your partner, a child, a relative, a friend, or even a pet. This is a being who evokes feelings of easy warmth and friendliness. Direct your loving-kindness thoughts there:

- *May you be safe and protected.*
- *May you be peaceful and at ease.*
- *May you feel joy.*
- *May you be well and strong.*
- *May you be free of fear and anxiety.*
- *May you be filled with loving kindness.*

Now think of a person you feel neutral about—a teller at the bank, your letter carrier, a stranger on the street. Direct the loving kindness toward him or her:

- *May you be well.*
- *May you be peaceful and at ease.*
- *May you be happy.*
- *May you be filled with loving kindness.*

Next, direct your thoughts toward people who may be causing you

discomfort or negative emotions and repeat the loving-kindness medita-
tion. Imagine that they are changed by these thoughts:

- *May you be well.*
- *May you be peaceful and at ease.*
- *May you be happy.*
- *May you be filled with loving kindness.*

Allow your feelings of loving kindness to grow in all directions,
touching people you know and even those you don't. Send your loving-
kindness thoughts to all humanity:

- *May you be well.*
- *May you be peaceful and at ease.*
- *May you be happy.*
- *May you be filled with loving kindness.*

Finish this meditation with five deep abdominal breaths.

Therapeutic Emotional Expression

RESOURCES FOR EMOTIONALLY EXPRESSIVE WRITING

James W. Pennebaker: http://homepage.psy.utexas.edu/ homepage/Faculty/Pennebaker/Home2000/JWPhome.htm
This website of one of the key researchers in the field includes relevant publications, research tools, and links.

Dr. Howard Schubiner's Mind Body Program: http://www. unlearnyourpain.com/index.php
This program uses expressive writing to help provide healthy expression of emotions to reduce pain and tension.

Center for Journal Therapy: www.journaltherapy.com/
The Center for Journal Therapy offers classes and instruction on using journaling for health.

My Therapy Journal: https://www.mytherapyjournal.com/
This online journal with secure entries provides multiple ways to express oneself. A fee is required.

HOW TO JOURNAL[1]

When working with stressful events:

1. Find a quiet place where you won't be disturbed.
2. Write about an upsetting or troubling experience in your life, something that has affected you deeply and that you have not discussed at length with others.
3. First describe the event in detail. Write about the situation, surroundings, and sensations that you remember.
4. Then describe your deepest feeling about the event. Let go and allow your emotions to run freely in your writing. Describe how you felt about the event then and how you feel about it now.
5. Write continuously. Don't worry about grammar, spelling, or sentence structure. If you come to a "block," simply repeat what you have already written.
6. Before finishing, write about what you may have learned or how you may have grown from the event.
7. Write for twenty minutes for at least four days. You can write about different events or reflect on the same one each day.
8. If the process proves helpful, consider keeping a journal regularly and/or sharing your feelings with someone you trust through a compassionate connection.

Acknowledgments

This book would not have been possible without the kind support of the Mental Insight Foundation. Their grant provided resources that allowed for its completion with the goal of creating an educational guide that would help shift society's focus from disease toward the healing potential within everyone.

Char Luchterhand, my longtime colleague at the University of Wisconsin, was pivotal in helping organize this and many projects that we worked on for more than a decade. Thanks Char!

I am grateful to Kate Ledger, a gifted writer who helped me get this book started. She introduced me to my literary agent, Laurie Abkemeier, who helped secure a publisher at W. W. Norton. I couldn't have navigated this new world without her. I am also grateful to Jill Bialosky, our editor at Norton, for her feedback and guidance, which helped make this a better book.

The stars aligned when they connected me to Susan Golant. Susan is a gifted writer who beautifully channels the person she is writing with, using her skills to make the message understandable and enjoyable. Thank you, Susan, for your partnership, mentoring, and friendship.

I am grateful to the teachers I have been blessed to learn from. Andrew Weil's commonsense genius helped me understand how to learn from and respect the wisdom of nature. Thanks to Jon Kabat-Zinn for introducing me to mindfulness, and a big thanks to Katharine Bonus, longtime director of the UW Mindfulness Program, who has filled me with all sorts of "ah-ha" moments through her gifted teaching style. Thanks to Tracy Gaudet for being there at the beginning of this Integrative Medicine journey and for the opportunity to work with shifting the VA health delivery system. Thanks to Rachel Naomi Remen for introducing me to the Healer's Art.

I am also very grateful to be part of an academic community of faculty and staff at the University of New Mexico who are dedicated to making this world a better place. I am honored to be able to work with you.

And most of all, to my patients, who have taught me so much over the years. It is such an honor to be able to make a living taking care of my friends.

—David Rakel, MD, Albuquerque, New Mexico

For my part, I am grateful to my agent, Madeleine Morel, for introducing me to David Rakel and to our editor at W. W. Norton, Jill Bialosky, for her insightful and cogent direction. Without them, this book would not have come to fruition. I'm also most grateful to David—one of the kindest and most compassionate human beings I've ever met. I feel blessed that he took me along on this journey of learning with him. And finally, as ever, I am grateful for my husband, Mitch Golant, himself a master of the compassionate connection and a constant source of strength, light, and love to me and our family.

—Susan K. Golant, MA, Los Angeles, California

Notes

INTRODUCTION

1. Empathy consists of this capacity to recognize another person's emotions and share. Empathy *training* activates centers of the brain (the anterior insula and midcingulate cortex) associated with pain and negative mood. See Chapter 10.
2. James K. Rilling et al., "A Neural Basis for Social Cooperation," *Neuron* 35, no. 2 (2002): 395–405.
3. Dacher Keltner, *Born to Be Good: The Science of a Meaningful Life* (New York: Norton, 2009), 6.

CHAPTER 1: COMPASSION HASTENS HEALING

1. Michael Balint, *The Doctor, His Patient and the Illness: Vol. 1* (New York: International Universities Press, 1957).
2. Frank Moriarty et al., "Trends and Interaction of Polypharmacy and Potentially Inappropriate Prescribing in Primary Care over 15 Years in Ireland: A Repeated Cross-Sectional Study," *BMJ Open* 5, no. 9 (2015): e008656.
3. Shelly L. Gray et al., "Cumulative Use of Strong Anticholinergics and Incident Dementia: A Prospective Cohort Study," *JAMA Internal Medicine* 175, no. 3 (2015): 401–7.
4. Martin Makary and Michael Daniel, "Medical Error—The Third Leading Cause of Death in the US," *BMJ* 353 (2016): i2139.
5. Keltner, *Born to Be Good*, 53–54.
6. See imconsortium.org.
7. Luana Colloca et al., "Overt versus Covert Treatment for Pain, Anxiety, and Parkinson's Disease," *Lancet Neurology* 3, no. 11 (2004): 679–84.
8. Tetsuo Koyama et al., "The Subjective Experience of Pain: Where

Expectations Become Reality," *Proceedings of the National Academy of Sciences of the United States of America* 102, no. 36 (2005): 12950–955.

9. Jodi Halpern, "What Is Clinical Empathy?' *Journal of General Internal Medicine* 18, no. 8 (2003): 670–74. doi:10.1046/j.1525-1497.2003.21017.x.

10. William Osler, *The Quotable Osler,* ed. Charles S. Bryan and Mark E. Silverman (Philadelphia: American College of Physicians, 2003).

11. Stefano Del Canale et al., "The Relationship between Physician Empathy and Disease Complications: An Empirical Study of Primary Care Physicians and Their Diabetic Patients in Parma, Italy," *Academic Medicine* 87, no. 9 (2012): 1243–49.

12. Ronald M. Epstein et al., "Patient-Centered Communication and Diagnostic Testing," *Annals of Family Medicine* 3, no. 5 (2005): 415–21.

13. Mohammadreza Hojat et al., "Physicians' Empathy and Clinical Outcomes for Diabetic Patients," *Academic Medicine* 86, no. 3 (2011): 359–64.

14. Bruce Barrett et al., "Echinacea for Treating the Common Cold: A Randomized Trial," *Annals of Internal Medicine* 153, no. 12 (2010): 769–77.

15. Bruce Barrett et al., "Placebo, Meaning, and Health," *Perspectives in Biology and Medicine* 49, no. 2 (2006): 178–98.

16. David P. Rakel, "Number 406, 'Standard'," *Family Medicine* 41, no. 4 (2009): 289–90.

17. David Rakel et al., "Perception of Empathy in the Therapeutic Encounter: Effects on the Common Cold," *Patient Education and Counseling* 85, no. 3 (2011): 390–97; David P. Rakel et al., "Practitioner Empathy and the Duration of the Common Cold," *Family Medicine* 41, no. 7 (2009): 494–501.

CHAPTER 2: THE MIND AND THE BODY—CONNECTED

1. Bruno Klopfer, "Psychological Variables in Human Cancer," *Journal of Projective Techniques,* no. 21 (1957): 331–40.

2. John A. Astin et al., "Barriers to the Integration of Psychosocial Factors in Medicine: Results of a National Survey of Physicians," *Journal of the American Board of Family Medicine* 19, no. 6 (2006): 557–65; Marianna Virtanen et al., "Psychological Distress and Incidence of Type 2 Diabetes in High-Risk and Low-Risk Populations: The Whitehall II Cohort Study," *Diabetes Care* 37, no. 8 (2014): 2091–97; Kieran C. Fox et al., "Is Meditation Associated with Altered Brain Structure? A Systematic Review and Meta-Analysis of Morphometric Neuroimaging in Meditation Practitioners," *Neuroscience and Biobehavioral Reviews* 43 (2014): 48–73.

3. http://vault.sierraclub.org/john_muir_exhibit/writings/misquotes. aspx.

4. David L. Sackett et al., "Evidence Based Medicine: What It Is and What It Isn't," *BMJ* 312, no. 7023 (1996): 71–72.

5. David Spiegel et al., "Effect of Psychosocial Treatment on Survival of Patients with Metastatic Breast Cancer," *Lancet* 2, no. 8668 (1989): 888–91.

6. Barbara L. Andersen et al., "Biobehavioral, Immune, and Health Benefits Following Recurrence for Psychological Intervention Participants," *Clinical Cancer Research* 16, no. 12 (2010): 3270–78.

7. In 2016 the name changed from the Institute of Medicine to Health and Medicine Division of the National Academies: http://www. nationalacademies.org/hmd/

8. Institute of Medicine, *Cancer Care for the Whole Patient: Meeting Psychosocial Health Needs*, ed. Nancy E. Adler and Ann E. K. Page (Washington, DC: National Academies Press, 2008).

9. See www.cancersupportcommunity.org for more information on the "patient active" concept.

10. Gray et al., "Use of Strong Anticholinergics."

11. Paul W. Andrews et al., "Blue Again: Perturbational Effects of Antidepressants Suggest Monoaminergic Homeostasis in Major Depression," *Frontiers in Psychology* 2 (2011): 159.

12. Michal Granot and Irit Weissman-Fogel, "The Effect of Post-Surgical Neuroplasticity on the Stability of Systemic Pain Perception: A Psychophysical Study," *European Journal of Pain* 16, no. 2 (2012): 247–55; Lucy Chen et al., "Altered Quantitative Sensory Testing Outcome in Subjects with Opioid Therapy," *Pain* 143, no. 1–2 (2009): 65–70.

13. Anna Niklasson et al., "Dyspeptic Symptom Development after Discontinuation of a Proton Pump Inhibitor: A Double-Blind Placebo-Controlled Trial," *American Journal of Gastroenterology* 105, no. 7 (2010): 1531–37.

14. Benjamin Lazarus et al., "Proton Pump Inhibitor Use and the Risk of Chronic Kidney Disease," *JAMA Internal Medicine* 176, no. 2 (2016): 238–46; Willy Gomm et al., "Association of Proton Pump Inhibitors with Risk of Dementia: A Pharmacoepidemiological Claims Data Analysis," *JAMA Neurology* 73, no. 4 (2016): 410–16; Nigam H. Shah et al., "Proton Pump Inhibitor Usage and the Risk of Myocardial Infarction in the General Population," *PLoS One* 10, no. 6 (2015): e0124653.

15. Inbal Golomb et al., "Long-Term Metabolic Effects of Laparoscopic Sleeve Gastrectomy," *JAMA Surgery* 150, no. 11 (2015): 1051–57.

16. Nicola Wiles et al., "Cognitive Behavioural Therapy as an Adjunct to Pharmacotherapy for Primary Care Based Patients with Treatment Resistant Depression: Results of the CoBalT Randomised Controlled Trial, *Lancet* 381, no. 9864 (2013): 375–84; Keith S. Dobson et al., "Randomized Trial of Behavioral Activation, Cognitive Therapy, and Antidepressant Medication in the Prevention of Relapse and Recurrence in Major Depression," *Journal of Consulting and Clinical Psychology* 76, no. 3 (2008): 468–77.

17. Jacob Piet and Esben Hougaard, "The Effect of Mindfulness-Based Cognitive Therapy for Prevention of Relapse in Recurrent Major Depressive Disorder: A Systematic Review and Meta-Analysis," *Clinical Psychology Review* 31, no. 6 (2011): 1032–40.

18. Marcelo M. Demarzo et al., "The Efficacy of Mindfulness-Based Interventions in Primary Care: A Meta-Analytic Review," *Annals of Family Medicine* 13, no. 6 (2015): 573–82; Rinske A. Gotink et al., "Standardised Mindfulness-Based Interventions in Healthcare: An Overview of Systematic Reviews and Meta-Analyses of RCTs," *PLoS One* 10, no. 4 (2015): e0124344.

19. Jon Kabat-Zinn et al., "Influence of a Mindfulness Meditation-Based Stress Reduction Intervention on Rates of Skin Clearing in Patients with Moderate to Severe Psoriasis Undergoing Phototherapy (UVB) and Photochemotherapy (PUVA)," *Psychosomatic Medicine* 60, no. 5 (1998): 625–32.

20. Thomas Jefferson, *The Writings of Thomas Jefferson*, ed. Paul Leicester Ford, vol. 9, 1799–1803 (New York: G. P. Putnam's Sons, 1898).

21. Brian Olshansky, "Placebo and Nocebo in Cardiovascular Health: Implications for Healthcare, Research, and the Doctor-Patient Relationship," *Journal of the American College of Cardiology* 49, no. 4 (2007): 415–21.

22. Raveendhara R. Bannuru et al., "Effectiveness and Implications of Alternative Placebo Treatments: A Systematic Review and Network Meta-Analysis of Osteoarthritis Trials," *Annals of Internal Medicine* 163, no. 5 (2015): 365–72, doi:10.7326/M15-0623.

23. Larry Dossey, "Telecebo: Beyond Placebo to an Expanded Concept of Healing," *Explore*, 12, no. 1 (2016): 1–12.

24. Kevin M. McKay, Zac E. Imel, and Bruce E. Wampold, "Psychiatrist Effects in the Psychopharmacological Treatment of Depression," *Journal of Affective Disorders* 92, no. 2–3 (2006): 287–90.

25. Pepijin D. Roelofs et al., "Nonsteroidal Anti-Inflammatory Drugs

for Low Back Pain: An Updated Cochrane Review," *Spine* 33, no. 16 (2008): 1766–74.

26. Jørgen Eriksen et al., "Critical Issues on Opioids in Chronic Non-Cancer Pain: An Epidemiological Study," *Pain* 125, no. 1–2 (2006): 172–79.

27. Cláudia Carvalho et al., "Open-Label Placebo Treatment in Chronic Low Back Pain: A Randomized Controlled Trial," *Pain* 157, no. 12 (2016): 2766–72.

28. Fabrizio Benedetti, Elisa Carlino, and Antonella Pollo, "How Placebos Change the Patient's Brain," *Neuropsychopharmacology* 36, no. 1 (2011): 339–54.

29. Tetsuo Koyama et al., "The Subjective Experience of Pain: Where Expectations Become Reality," *Proceedings of the National Academy of Sciences of the United States of America* 102, no. 36 (2005): 12950–55.

CHAPTER 3: THE BIOLOGY OF CONNECTION

1. Jacobo Grinberg-Zylberbaum et al., "The Einstein-Podolsky-Rosen Paradox in the Brain: The Transferred Potential," *Physics Essays* 7, no. 4 (1994): 422–28; Jacobo Grinberg-Zylberbaum et al., "Human Shared Potential and Activity of the Brain," *Subtle Energies* 3, no. 3 (1993): 25–43.

2. Jeanne Achterberg et al., "Evidence for Correlations between Distant Intentionality and Brain Function in Recipients: A Functional Magnetic Resonance Imaging Analysis," *Journal of Alternative and Complementary Medicine* 11, no. 6 (2005): 965–71.

3. Rita Pizzi et al., *Non-Local Correlation between Separated Neural Networks*, ed. E. Donkor, A. R. Pirick, and H. E. Brandt (Orlando, FL: Quantum Information and Computation II, 2004), 107–17.

4. Ashkan Farhadi et al., "Evidence for Non-Chemical, Non-Electrical Intercellular Signaling in Intestinal Epithelial Cells," *Bioelectrochemistry* 71, no. 2 (2007): 142–48.

5. Rollin McCraty et al., "The Electricity of Touch: Detection and Measurement of Cardiac Energy Exchange between People," in *Brain and Values: Is a Biological Science of Values Possible?* ed. Karl H. Pribram (Mahwah, NJ: Lawrence Erlbaum Associates, 1998), 359–79.

6. Tiffany Field, "Relationships as Regulators," *Psychology* 3, no. 6 (2012): 467–79.

7. David C. McClelland and Carol Kirshnit, "The Effect of Motivational Arousal through Films on Salivary Immunoglobulin A," *Psychology & Health* 2, no. 1 (1988): 31–52.

8. Ella A. Cooper et al., "You Turn Me Cold: Evidence for Temperature Contagion," *PLoS One* 9, no. 12 (2014): e116126.

9. Vittorio Gallese, Morris N. Eagle, and Paolo Migone, "Intentional Attunement: Mirror Neurons and the Neural Underpinnings of Interpersonal Relations," *Journal of the American Psychoanalytic Association* 55, no. 1 (2007): 131–75.

10. Giacomo Rizzolati and Laila Craighero, "The Mirror-Neuron System," *Annual Review of Neuroscience* 27 (2004): 169–92; Marco Iacoboni et al., "Cortical Mechanisms of Human Imitation," *Science* 286, no. 5449 (1999): 2526–28.

11. Guillaume Dumas et al., "Inter-Brain Synchronization during Social Interaction," *PLoS ONE* 5, no. 8 (2010): e12166, doi:10.1371/journal.pone.0012166.

12. Pier Francesco Ferrari and Giacomo Rizzolatti, "Mirror Neuron Research: The Past and the Future," *Philosophical Transactions of the Royal Society B* 369, no. 1644 (2014): 20130169, doi:10.1098/rstb.2013.0169.

13. Pier Francesco Ferrari, "The Neuroscience of Social Relations: A Comparative-Based Approach to Empathy and to the Capacity of Evaluating Others' Action Value," *Behaviour* 151, no. 2–3 (2014): 297–313, doi:10.1163/1568539X-00003152.

14. Paula M. Niedenthal et al., "Embodiment in Attitudes, Social Perception, and Emotion," *Personality and Social Psychology Review* 9, no. 3 (2005): 184–211.

15. Nicholas A. Christakis and James H. Fowler, *Connected: The Surprising Power of Our Social Networks and How They Shape Our Lives* (New York: Back Bay Books, 2011).

16. Maria Blackburn, "Shockney Therapy," *Johns Hopkins Magazine* 60, no. 2 (2008), http://pages.jh.edu/jhumag/0408web/shockney.html.

17. Dana R. Carney, Amy J. C. Cuddy, and Andy J. Yap, "Power Posing: Brief Nonverbal Displays Affect Neuroendocrine Levels and Risk Tolerance," *Psychological Science* 21, no. 10 (2010): 1363–68, doi:10.1177/0956797610383437.

18. Sarah Blaffer Hrdy and C. Sue Carter, "Hormonal Cocktails for Two," *Natural History* 104, no. 12 (1995): 34.

19. Izelle Labuschangne et al., "Oxytocin Attenuates Amygdala Reactivity to Fear in Generalized Social Anxiety Disorder," *Neuropsychopharmacology* 35, no. 12 (2010): 2403–13; Deborah Brauser, "Intranasal Oxytocin: The End of Fear?" *Medscape*, November 7, 2014, http://www.medscape.com/viewarticle/834585.

20. Kathleen C. Light, Karen M. Grewen, and Janet A. Amico, "More Fre-

quent Partner Hugs and Higher Oxytocin Levels Are Linked to Lower Blood Pressure and Heart Rate in Premenopausal Women," *Biological Psychology* 69, no. 1 (2005): 5–21, Epub December 29, 2004.

21. James McIntosh, " 'Love Hormone' Nasal Spray Could Reduce Calorie Intake in Men," *Medical News Today*, March 9, 2015.

22. Shelley E. Taylor, "Tend and Befriend: Biobehavioral Bases of Affiliation under Stress," *Current Directions in Psychological Science* 15, no. 6 (2006): 273–77.

23. Simon Kessner et al., "Effect of Oxytocin on Placebo Analgesia: A Randomized Study," *JAMA* 310, no. 16 (2013): 1733–34.

24. Sheldon Cohen et al., "Sociability and Susceptibility to the Common Cold," *Psychological Science* 14, no. 5 (2003): 389–95.

25. Sheldon Cohen et al., "Does Hugging Provide Stress-Buffering Social Support? A Study of Susceptibility to Upper Respiratory Infection and Illness," *Psychological Science* 26, no. 2 (2015): 135–47, doi:10.1177/0956797614559284.

26. Richard J. Davidson and Sharon Begley, *The Emotional Life of Your Brain: How Its Unique Patterns Affect the Way You Think, Feel, and Live— and How You Can Change Them* (New York: Plume, 2012), 167.

27. Edward Taub et al., "A Placebo-Controlled Trail of Constraint-Induced Movement Therapy for Upper Extremity after Stroke," *Stroke* 37, no. 4 (2007): 1045–49.

28. http://www.ncbi.nlm.nih.gov/pmc/articles/PMC1738559/,http://www .cogneurosociety.org/brain-rewire-after-surgery/,andhttp://www.scien tificamerican.com/article/strange-but-true-when-half-brain-better-than-whole/.

29. Alvaro Pascual-Leone et al., "The Plastic Human Brain Cortex," *Annual Review of Neuroscience* 28 (2005): 377–401.

30. A. Vania Apkarian et al., "Chronic Back Pain Is Associated with Decreased Prefrontal and Thalamic Gray Matter Density," *Journal of Neuroscience* 24, no. 46 (2004): 10410–15.

31. Floris P. de Lange et al., "Increase in Prefrontal Cortical Volume Following Cognitive Behavioural Therapy in Patients with Chronic Fatigue Syndrome," *Brain* 131, pt. 8 (2008): 2172–80.

32. Davidson and Begley, *Life of Your Brain*, 172.

33. Richard J. Davidson et al., "Alterations in Brain and Immune Function Produced by Mindfulness Meditation," *Psychosomatic Medicine* 65, no. 4 (2003): 564–70.

34. Tait D. Shanafelt et al., "Changes in Burnout and Satisfaction with Work-Life Balance in Physicians and the General US Working Popula-

tion between 2011 and 2014," *Mayo Clinic Proceedings* 90, no. 12 (2015): 1600–1613.

35. "Epigenetics: What Makes a Queen Bee?" *Nature* 468, no. 348 (November 18, 2010): 348, doi:10.1038/468348a.

36. Danielle L. Champagne et al., "Maternal Care and Hippocampal Plasticity: Evidence for Experience-Dependent Structural Plasticity, Altered Synaptic Functioning, and Differential Responsiveness to Glucocorticoids and Stress," *Journal of Neuroscience* 28, no. 23 (2008): 6037–45.

37. Tie-Yuan Zhang and Michael J. Meany, "Epigenetics and the Environmental Regulation of the Genome and Its Function," *Annual Review of Psychology* 61 (2010): 439–66.

38. Dean Ornish et al., "Intensive Lifestyle Changes May Affect the Progression of Prostate Cancer," *Journal of Urology* 174, no. 3 (2005): 1065–70, doi:10.1097/01.ju.0000169487.49018.73.

39. Evadnie Rampersaud et al., "Physical Activity and the Association of Common FTO Gene Variants with Body Mass Index and Obesity," *Archives of Internal Medicine* 168, no. 16 (2008): 1791–97.

40. James Niels Rosenquist et al., "Cohort of Birth Modifies the Association between FTO Genotype and BMI," *Proceedings of the National Academy of Sciences of the United States of America* 112, no. 2 (2014): 354–59.

41. Keltner, *Born to Be Good*, 228.

42. J. Kiley Hamlin, Karen Wynn, and Paul Bloom, "Three-Month-Olds Show a Negativity Bias in Their Social Evaluations," *Developmental Science* 13, no. 6 (2010): 923–29.

43. Rilling, "Basis for Social Cooperation," 395–405.

44. Stephen W. Porges, "Orienting in a Defensive World: Mammalian Modifications of Our Evolutionary Heritage. A Polyvagal Theory," *Psychophysiology* 32, no. 4 (1995): 301–18.

45. Jennifer E. Stellar et al., "Affective and Physiological Responses to the Suffering of Others: Compassion and Vagal Activity," *Journal of Personality and Social Psychology* 108, no. 4 (2015): 572–85.

46. Keltner, *Born to Be Good*, 239–40.

CHAPTER 4: MAKE HEALTH PRIMARY

1. Viktor Frankl, *Man's Search for Meaning* (Boston: Beacon Press, 2006).

2. Aaron Antonovsky et al., "Twenty-Five Years Later: A Limited Study of the Sequelae of the Concentration Camp Experience," *Social Psychiatry* 6, no. 4 (1971): 186–93.

3. Philip Brickman, Dan Coates, and Ronnie Janoff-Bulman, "Lottery Winners and Accident Victims: Is Happiness Relative? *Journal of Personality and Social Psychology* 36, no. 8 (1978): 917–27.

4. Rehab medicine/strong spiritual beliefs.

5. Vincent J. Felitti et al., "Relationship of Childhood Abuse and Household Dysfunction to Many of the Leading Causes of Death in Adults: The Adverse Childhood Experiences (ACE) Study," *American Journal of Preventive Medicine* 14, no. 4 (1998): 245–58.

6. Rosalynn Carter, Susan K. Golant, and Kathryn E. Cade, *Within Our Reach: Ending the Mental Health Crisis* (New York: Rodale, 2010).

7. Karen Rodham, Nicola Rance, and David Blake, "A Qualitative Exploration of Carers' and 'Patients' Experiences of Fibromyalgia: One Illness, Different Perspectives," *Musculoskeletal Care* 8, no. 2 (2010): 68–77.

8. Ibid.

9. Antoine Louveau et al., "Structural and Functional Features of Central Nervous System Lymphatic Vessels," *Nature* 523, no. 7560 (2015): 337–41.

10. Kristen B. Thomas, "General Practice Consultations: Is There Any Point in Being Positive? *British Medical Journal (Clinical Research Edition)* 294, no. 6581 (1987): 1200–1202.

11. Robert Rosenthal and Lenore Jacobson, "Pygmalion in the Classroom," *Urban Review* 3, no. 1 (1968): 16–20.

12. Robert Rosenthal and Donald B. Rubin, "Interpersonal Expectancy Effects: The First 345 Studies," *Behavioral and Brain Sciences* 1, no. 3 (1978): 377–86.

13. Joseph Jastrow, *Fact and Fable in Psychology* (Boston: Houghton Mifflin, 1900).

CHAPTER 5: GOOD INTENTIONS GONE BAD

1. Davidson and Begley, *Emotional Life of Your Brain*, 222.

2. Sandra G. Boodman, "How to Teach Doctors Empathy," *The Atlantic*, March 15, 2015, http://www.theatlantic.com/health/archive/2015/03/how-to-teach-doctors-empathy/387784/.

3. Thomas Luparello et al., "Influences of Suggestion on Airway Reactivity in Asthmatic Subjects," *Psychosomatic Medicine* 30, no. 6 (1968): 819–25.

4. C. Warren Olanow et al., "A Double-Blind Controlled Trial of Bilateral Fetal Nigral Transplantation in Parkinson's Disease," *Annals of Neurology* 54, no. 3 (2003): 403–14; Curt R. Freed et al., "Transplantation of Embryonic Dopamine Neurons for Severe Parkinson's Disease," *New England Journal of Medicine* 344, no. 10 (2001): 710–19.

5. Walter B. Cannon, "Voodoo Death," *American Anthropologist* 44, no. 2 (1942): 169.

6. Ibid., 172.

7. Esther M. Sternberg, "Walter B. Cannon and '"Voodoo" Death': A Per-

spective from 60 Years On," *American Journal of Public Health* 92, no. 10 (2002): 1564–66.

8. Rebecca Voelker, "Nocebos Contribute to a Host of Ills," *JAMA* 275, no. 5 (1996): 345–47.

9. Ilan S. Wittstein et al., "Neurohumoral Features of Myocardial Stunning Due to Sudden Emotional Stress," *New England Journal of Medicine* 352, no. 6 (2005): 539–48.

10. Christian Templin et al., "Clinical Features and Outcomes of Takotsubo (Stress) Cardiomyopathy," *New England Journal of Medicine* 373, no. 10 (2015): 929–38.

11. http://www.nytimes.com/2003/04/26/opinion/the-monk-in-the-lab.html.

CHAPTER 6: IDENTIFY AND FREE YOURSELF OF YOUR BIASES

1. Anaïs Nin, *The Diary of Anaïs Nin, 1939–1944* (New York: Harcourt Brace & World, 1969).

2. Trafton Drew, Melissa L.-H. Võ, and Jeremy M. Wolfe, "The Invisible Gorilla Strikes Again: Sustained Inattentional Blindness in Expert Observers," *Psychological Science* 24, no. 9 (2013): 1848–53.

3. H. G. Schmidt et al., "Do Patients' Disruptive Behaviours Influence the Accuracy of a Doctor's Diagnosis? A Randomised Experiment," *BMJ Quality and Safety* 26 (2016): 19–23.

4. Silvia Mamede et al., "Why Patients' Disruptive Behaviours Impair Diagnostic Reasoning: A Randomised Experiment," *BMJ Quality and Safety* 26, no. 1 (2016): 13–18, doi:10.1136/bmjqs-2015-005065 [Epub ahead of print].

5. Deborah Dang et al., "Do Clinician Disruptive Behaviors Make an Unsafe Environment for Patients?" *Journal of Nursing Care Quality* 31, no. 2 (2016): 115–23.

6. David S. Rakel and Daniel Shapiro, "Mind-Body Medicine," in *Textbook of Family Medicine*, 6th ed., ed. Robert E. Rakel (Philadelphia: W. B. Saunders, 2002), 54.

7. Ronald M. Epstein, "Mindful Practice," *JAMA* 282, no. 9 (1999): 833–39.

8. David L. Rosenhan, "On Being Sane in Insane Places," *Science* 179, no. 70 (1973): 250–58.

CHAPTER 7: BE PRESENT, ON PURPOSE, WITHOUT JUDGMENT

1. Anthony L. Suchman et al., "A Model of Empathic Communication in the Medical Interview," *JAMA* 277, no. 8 (1997): 678–82.

2. Ronald M. Epstein, "Mindful Practice," *JAMA* 282, no. 9 (1999): 833–39.

3. Katharine A. Atwood et al., "Impact of a Clinical Educational Effort in Driving Transformation in Healthcare," *Family Medicine* 48, no. 9 (2016): 711–19.

4. Charlene Luchterhand et al., "Creating a Culture of Mindfulness in Medicine," *Wisconsin Medical Journal* 114, no. 3 (2015): 105–9; Mary Catherine Beach et al., "A Multicenter Study of Physician Mindfulness and Health Care Quality," *Annals of Family Medicine* 11, no. 5 (2013): 421–28.

5. Olga M. Klimecki et al., "Differential Pattern of Functional Brain Plasticity after Compassion and Empathy Training," *Social Cognitive and Affective Neuroscience* 9, no. 6 (2014): 873–79.

6. Ricard Matthieu, Antoine Lutz, and Richard J. Davidson, "Mind of the Meditator," *Scientific American* 311, no. 5 (2014): 38–45.

7. Britta K. Hölzel et al., "Mindfulness Practice Leads to Increases in Regional Brain Gray Matter Density," *Psychiatry Research* 191, no. 1 (2011): 36–43.

8. Luke Fortney et al., "Abbreviated Mindfulness Intervention for Job Satisfaction, Quality of Life, and Compassion in Primary Care Clinicians: A Pilot Study," *Annals of Family Medicine* 11, no. 5 (2013): 412–20.

9. John Makransky, "Compassion beyond Fatigue: Contemplative Training for People Who Serve Others" (unpublished manuscript, 2015). "Compassion beyond Fatigue" workshops are listed at www.johnmakransky.org and "workshops and retreats" at http://foundationforactivecompassion.com/. See also Makransky's book *Awakening through Love: Unveiling Your Deepest Goodness* (Somerville, MA: Wisdom, 2007) for a fuller explanation of the meditations and how they were adapted from Tibetan praxis. He developed these techniques over nine years while teaching in meditation retreats sponsored by Dzogchen Center (www.dzogchen.org), and at the Barre Center for Buddhist Studies (www.dharma.org/bcbs) and Rangjung Yeshe Gomde Austria (www.gomde.de/eng/).

10. Matthew A. Killingsworth and Daniel T. Gilbert, "A Wandering Mind Is an Unhappy Mind," *Science* 330, no. 6006 (2010): 932.

11. Howard B. Beckman and Richard Frankel, "The Effect of Physician Behavior on the Collection of Data," *Annals of Internal Medicine* 101, no. 5 (1984): 692–96; Wolf Langewitz et al., "Spontaneous Talking Time at Start of Consultation in Outpatient Clinic: Cohort Study," *BMJ* 325, no. 7366 (2002): 682–83.

12. M. Kim Marvel et al., "Soliciting the Patient's Agenda: Have We Improved?" *JAMA* 281, no. 3 (1999): 283–87.

13. Edward Krupat et al., "When Physicians and Patients Think Alike: Patient-Centered Beliefs and Their Impact on Satisfaction and Trust," *Journal of Family Practice* 50, no. 12 (2001): 1057–62.

14. Elizabeth Toll, "A Piece of My Mind. The Cost of Technology," *JAMA* 307, no. 23 (2012): 2497–98.

15. Christine A. Sinsky and John W. Beasley, "Texting While Doctoring: A Patient Safety Hazard," *Annals of Internal Medicine* 160, no. 8 (2014): 583–84.

CHAPTER 8: PHYSICALLY COMMUNICATE GOOD INTENTIONS

1. Ann G. Carmichael and Richard M. Ratzan, eds., *Medicine: A Treasury of Art and Literature* (New York: Hugh Lauter Levin Associates, 1991). Anonymous admonitions of Hippocrates of learning the history of medicine, 53–54.

2. Audrey Nelson and Susan K. Golant, *You Don't Say: Navigating Nonverbal Communication between the Sexes* (New York: Berkley Publishing Group, 2004), 2–3.

3. Alice Mado Proverbio et al., "Comprehending Body Language and Mimics: An ERP and Neuroimaging Study on Italian Actors and Viewers," *PLoS One* 9, no. 3 (2014): e91294.

4. Kelli J. Swayden et al., "Effect of Sitting vs. Standing on Perception of Provider Time at Bedside: A Pilot Study," *Patient Education and Counseling* 86, no. 2 (2012): 166–71; Graham Jackson, "'Oh . . . by the Way . . .': Doorknob Syndrome," *International Journal of Clinical Practice* 59, no. 8 (2005): 869.

5. Florian Strasser et al., "Impact of Physician Sitting versus Standing during Inpatient Oncology Consultations: Patients' Preference and Perception of Compassion and Duration. A Randomized Controlled Trial," *Journal of Pain and Symptom Management* 29, no. 5 (2005): 489–97.

6. Dana R. Carney, Amy J. C. Cuddy, and Andy J. Yap, "Power Posing: Brief Nonverbal Displays Affect Neuroendocrine Levels and Risk Tolerance," *Psychological Science* 21, no. 10 (2010): 1363–68.

7. Bernard Lown, *The Lost Art of Healing* (Boston: Houghton Mifflin, 1996), 10.

8. Rakel, "Mind-Body Medicine," 54.

9. Paul Ekman, "Darwin, Deception, and Facial Expression," *Annals of the New York Academy of Sciences* 1000, no. 1 (2003): 205–21.

10. Jerry D. Boucher and Paul Ekman, "Facial Areas and Emotional Information," *Journal of Communication* 25, no. 2 (1975): 21–29; Paul Ekman, *Darwin and Facial Expression* (Cambridge, MA: Malor Books, 2006).

11. Allan Pease and Barbara Pease, *The Definitive Book of Body Language* (New York: Bantam, 2004).

12. David Lewis, *The Secret Languages of Success: Using Body Language to Get What You Want* (New York: Galahad, 1989).

13. Larry R. Churchill and David Schenck, "Healing Skills for Medical Practice," *Annals of Internal Medicine* 149, no. 10 (2008): 720–24.

14. Frans de Waal, *Peacemaking among Primates* (Cambridge, MA: Harvard University Press, 1989).

15. Guillaume-Benjamin Duchenne, *The Mechanism of Human Facial Expression* (New York: Cambridge University Press, 1862), trans. R. Andrew Cuthbertson (New York: Cambridge University Press, 1990); Marianne LaFrance, *Why Smile: The Science Behind Facial Expressions* (New York: W. W. Norton, 2011).

16. Paul Ekman and Erika L. Rosenberg, eds., *What the Face Reveals: Basic and Applied Studies of Spontaneous Expression Using the Facial Action Coding System (FACS)* (New York: Oxford University Press, 2005).

17. Flora Davis, *Inside Intuition: What We Know about Nonverbal Communication* (New York: New American Library, 1975).

18. Rakel, "Mind-Body Medicine."

19. Albert Mehrabian, *Silent Messages: Implicit Communication of Emotions and Attitudes*, 2nd ed. (Belmont, CA: Wadsworth, 1981).

20. April H. Crusco and Christopher G. Wetzel, "The Midas Touch: The Effects of Interpersonal Touch on Restaurant Tipping," *Personality and Social Psychology Bulletin* 10, no. 4 (1984): 512–17.

21. Nelson and Golant, *You Don't Say*, 120.

22. Susan M. Ludington-Hoe with Susan K. Golant, *Kangaroo Care: The Best You Can Do to Help Your Preterm Infant* (New York: Bantam, 1993).

23. Desmond Morris, *Manwatching: A Field Guide to Human Behavior* (New York: Abrams, 1977).

24. Pease and Pease, *Book of Body Language*.

CHAPTER 9: SEEK ANOTHER PERSON'S AUTHENTIC STORY

1. Thich Nhat Hanh, *Living Buddha, Living Christ* (New York: Riverhead Books, 1995).

2. George A. Miller, "Insights and Outlooks," *Journal of Applied Behavioral Science* 5, no. 2 (1969): 275–78.

3. Michael Stein, "We All Want Our Doctors to Be Kind. But Does Kindness

Actually Help Us Get Well?" *Washington Post*, August 11, 2016, https://www.washingtonpost.com/opinions/we-all-want-our-doctors-to-be-kind-but-does-kindness-actually-help-us-get-well/2016/08/11/95306e06-1091-11e6-8967-7ac733c56f12_story.html?utm_term=.13a2b9fce209.

4. CRICO Strategies, *Malpractice Risks in Communication Failures: 2015. Annual Benchmarking Report.*

5. Melissa Bailey, "Communication Failures Linked to 1,744 Deaths in Five Years, US Malpractice Study Finds," *Pulse of Longwood*, February 2016.

6. http://www.nytimes.com/2015/12/03/us/politics/health-spending-in-us-topped-3-trillion-last-year.html?smprod=nytcore-iphone&smid=nytcore-iphone-share&_r=0.

7. Matthias R. Mehl et al., "Eavesdropping on Happiness: Well-Being Is Related to Having Less Small Talk and More Substantive Conversations," *Psychological Science* 21, no. 4 (2010): 539–41.

8. Diane S. Berry and James W. Pennebaker, "Nonverbal and Verbal Emotional Expression and Health," *Psychotherapy and Psychosomatics* 59, no. 1 (1993): 11–19.

9. James W. Pennebaker, *Opening Up: The Healing Power of Expressing Emotions* (New York: Guilford Press, 1997).

10. Janine K. Kiecolt-Glaser et al., "Marital Stress: Immunologic, Neuroendocrine, and Autonomic Correlates," *Annals of the New York Academy of Sciences* 840 (1998): 656–63.

11. Adrienne Hampton and David Rakel, "Journaling for Health," in *Integrative Medicine*, 4th ed., ed. David Rakel (Philadelphia: Elsevier, 2017).

12. Michael A. Cohn, Matthias R. Mehl, and James W. Pennebaker, "Linguistic Markers of Psychological Change Surrounding September 11, 2001," *Psychological Science* 15, no. 10 (2004): 687–93.

13. David P. Rakel, "Journaling: The Effects of Disclosure on Health," *Alternative Medical Alert* 7 (2004): 8–11.

14. Joshua M. Smyth et al., "Effects of Writing about Stressful Experiences on Symptom Reduction in Patients with Asthma or Rheumatoid Arthritis," *JAMA* 281, no. 14 (1999): 1304–09.

15. Mark A. Lumley et al., "Does Emotional Disclosure about Stress Improve Health in Rheumatoid Arthritis? Randomized, Controlled Trials of Written and Spoken Disclosure," *Pain* 152, no. 4 (2011): 866–77.

16. Henriët van Middendorp et al., "Health and Physiological Effects of an Emotional Disclosure Intervention Adapted for Application at

Home: A Randomized Clinical Trial in Rheumatoid Arthritis," *Psychotherapy and Psychosomatics* 78, no. 3 (2009): 145–51.

17. Joan E. Broderick, Doerte U. Junghaenel, and Joseph E. Schwartz, "Written Emotional Expression Produces Health Benefits in Fibromyalgia Patients," *Psychosomatic Medicine* 67, no. 2 (2005): 326–34.

18. Mazy E. Gilli et al., "The Health Effects of At-Home Written Emotional Disclosure in Fibromyalgia: A Randomized Trial," *Annals of Behavioral Medicine* 32, no. 2 (2006): 135–46.

19. Jessica Walburn et al., "Psychological Stress and Wound Healing in Humans: A Systematic Review and Meta-Analysis," *Journal of Psychosomatic Research* 67, no. 3 (2009): 253–71.

20. Hannah Maple et al., "Stress Predicts the Trajectory of Wound Healing in Living Kidney Donors as Measured by High-Resolution Ultrasound," *Brain, Behavior, and Immunity* 43, (2015): 19–26.

21. John Weinman et al., "Enhanced Wound Healing after Emotional Disclosure Intervention," *British Journal of Health Psychology* 13, no. 1 (2008): 95–102; C. L. Banburey, "Wounds Heal More Quickly If Patients Are Relieved of Stress: A Review of Research by Susanne Scott and Colleagues from King's College, London." Presented at the Annual Conference of the British Psychological Society, *BMJ* 327 (2003): 522.

22. James W. Pennebaker, Tracy J. Mayne, and Martha E. Francis, "Linguistic Predictors of Adaptive Bereavement," *Journal of Personality and Social Psychology* 72, no. 4 (1997): 863–71; James W. Pennebaker, "Pain, Language, and Healing" (Presented at the Biofeedback Society of Wisconsin Integrative Health-Care Conference, Green Lake, WI, September 11–13, 2003).

23. Diane Boinon et al., "Changes in Psychological Adjustment over the Course of Treatment for Breast Cancer: The Predictive Role of Social Sharing and Social Support, *Psycho-Oncology* 23, no. 3 (2014): 291–98.

24. Stephen Covey, *The 7 Habits of Highly Successful People* (New York: Simon & Schuster, 2004).

25. Ideally, helpers should limit their interruptions to those times when they must change the subject, explain a problem, draw out more information if the person has not been forthcoming, provide encouragement, or address and diminish a patient's apprehensions.

26. Howard B. Beckman and Richard M. Frankel, "The Effect of Physician Behavior on the Collection of Data," *Annals of Internal Medicine* 101, no. 5 (1984): 692–96.

27. Jackson, "Doorknob Syndrome," 869.
28. http://www.oprah.com/spirit/oprah-talks-to-thich-nhat-hanh#ixzz4n 7gItxNQ.
29. Dimitrius and Mazzarella, 1999. https://www.amazon.com/Reading -People-Understand-Behavior-Anytime-Anyplace/dp/0345504135.
30. Irving Kirsch et al., "Initial Severity and Antidepressant Benefits: A Meta-Analysis of Data Submitted to the Food and Drug Administration," *PLoS Medicine* 5, no. 2 (2008): e45; Jay C. Fournier et al., "Antidepressant Drug Effects and Depression Severity: A Patient-Level Meta-Analysis," *JAMA* 303, no. 1 (2010): 47–53.
31. Nigam H. Shah et al., "Proton Pump Inhibitor Usage and the Risk of Myocardial Infarction in the General Population," *PLoS One* 10, no. 6 (2015): e0124653.
32. Benjamin Lazarus et al., "Proton Pump Inhibitor Use and the Risk of Chronic Kidney Disease," *JAMA Internal Medicine* 176, no. 2 (2016): 238–46.
33. Willy Gomm et al., "Association of Proton Pump Inhibitors with Risk of Dementia: A Pharmacoepidemiological Claims Data Analysis," *JAMA Neurology* 73, no. 4 (2016): 410–16.
34. Ronald M. Epstein et al., "Patient-Centered Communication and Diagnostic Testing," *Annals of Family Medicine* 3, no. 5 (2005): 415–21.
35. Eric B. Larson and Xin Yao, "Clinical Empathy as Emotional Labor in the Patient-Physician Relationship," *JAMA* 293, no. 9 (2005): 1100–106.
36. Mitch Golant and Susan K. Golant, *What to Do When Someone You Love Is Depressed: A Self-Help and Help-Others Guide* (New York: Henry Holt, 2007), 88.
37. Wolf Langewitz et al., "Spontaneous Talking Time at Start of Consultation in Outpatient Clinic: Cohort Study," *BMJ* 325, no. 7366 (2002): 682–83.

CHAPTER 10: MOVE FROM BURNOUT TOWARD BEAUTY

1. Hafiz, excerpt from *Love Poems from God: Twelve Sacred Voices from the East and West* by Daniel Ladinsky, copyright 2002.
2. Rosalynn Carter with Susan K. Golant, *Helping Yourself Help Others: A Book for Caregivers*, rev. ed. (New York: Public Affairs, 2013), 3.
3. MetLife Mature Market Institute, *MetLife Study of Caregiving Costs to Working Caregivers: Double Jeopardy for Baby Boomers Caring for Their Parents*, June 2011, https://www.metlife.com/mmi/research/caregiving-cost-working-caregivers.html#keyfindings.June.

4. Carter with Golant, *Helping Yourself Help Others.*
5. MetLife Mature Market Institute, *Study of Caregiving Costs.*
6. Tait D. Shanafelt et al., "Changes in Burnout and Satisfaction with Work-Life Balance in Physicians and the General US Working Population between 2011 and 2014," *Mayo Clinic Proceedings* 90, no. 12 (2015): 1600–13.
7. John M. Kelley et al., "The Influence of the Patient-Clinician Relationship on Healthcare Outcomes: A Systematic Review and Meta-Analysis of Randomized Controlled Trials," *PLoS One* 9, no. 4 (2014): e94207; Helen Riess et al., "Empathy Training for Resident Physicians: A Randomized Controlled Trial of a Neuroscience-Informed Curriculum," *Journal of General Internal Medicine* 27, no. 10 (2012): 1280–86.
8. Liselotte N. Dyrbye et al., "Relationship between Burnout and Professional Conduct and Attitudes among US Medical Students," *JAMA* 304, no. 11 (2010): 1173–80.
9. Olga M. Klimecki et al., "Differential Pattern of Functional Brain Plasticity after Compassion and Empathy Training," *Social Cognitive and Affective Neuroscience* 9, no. 6 (2014): 873–79.
10. Ibid.
11. Ibid.
12. Tania Singer and Olga M. Klimecki, "Empathy and Compassion," *Current Biology* 24, no. 18 (2014): R875–78.
13. Herbert J. Freudenberger, "Recognizing and Dealing with Burnout," in *The Professional and Family Caregiver—Dilemmas, Rewards, and New Directions,* eds. Jack A. Nottingham and Joanne Nottingham (Americus, GA: Rosalynn Carter Institute for Human Development, Georgia Southwest College, 1990).
14. Matthieu Ricard, Antoine Lutz, and Richard J. Davidson, "The Mind of the Meditator," *Scientific American* 311, no. 5 (2014): 38–45.
15. Singer and Klimecki, "Empathy and Compassion."
16. Glen Rein, Mike Atkinson, and Rollin McCraty, "The Physiological and Psychological Effects of Compassion and Anger," *Journal of Advancement in Medicine* 8 (1995): 87–105.
17. Klimecki et al., "Pattern of Brain Plasticity."
18. Michael J. Poulin, "Volunteering Predicts Health among Those Who Value Others: Two National Studies," *Health Psychology,* 33, no. 2 (2014): 120–29, http://dx.doi.org/10.1037/a0031620.
19. Tristen K. Inagaki and Naomi I. Eisenberger, "Neural Correlates of Giving Support to a Loved One," *Psychosomatic Medicine* 74, no. 1 (2012): 3–7.
20. Rein, Atkinson, and McCraty, "Compassion and Anger," 87–105.

21. Ibid.

22. David P. Rakel and Adam Rindfleisch, "Inflammation: Nutritional, Botanical, and Mind-Body Influences," *Southern Medical Journal* 98, no. 3 (2005): 303–10.

23. Anna Friis et al., "Kindness Matters: A Randomized Controlled Trial of a Mindful Self-Compassion Intervention Improves Depression, Distress, and HbA1c among Patients with Diabetes," *Diabetes Care* 39, no. 11 (2016): 1963–71.

24. Thaddeus W. W. Pace et al., "Effect of Compassion Meditation on Neuroendocrine, Innate Immune and Behavioral Responses to Psychosocial Stress," *Psychoneuroendocrinology* 34, no. 1 (2009): 87–98; Perla Kaliman et al., "Rapid Changes in Histone Deacetylases and Inflammatory Gene Expression in Expert Meditators," *Psychoneuroendocrinology* 40 (2014): 96–107.

25. Klimecki et al., "Pattern of Brain Plasticity," 873–79.

26. Lorenza S. Colzato, Ayca Ozturk, and Bernhard Hommel, "Meditate to Create: The Impact of Focused-Attention and Open-Monitoring Training on Convergent and Divergent Thinking," *Frontiers in Psychology* 3 (2012): 116.

27. Philip Goldberg, *The Intuitive Edge: Understanding and Developing Intuition* (Los Angeles: J. P. Tarcher, 1983).

APPENDIX B: THERAPEUTIC EMOTIONAL EXPRESSION

1. Adapted from David P. Rakel and Daniel Shapiro, "Mind-Body Medicine," in *Textbook of Family Medicine*, 6th ed., ed. Robert E. Rakel (Philadelphia: W. B. Saunders, 2002).

Index

Note: Page numbers in *italics* refer to illustrations.

About the Authors

Dr. David Rakel started his career near the Teton Mountains in Driggs, Idaho, where he was in rural private practice for five years before completing a two-year residential fellowship in integrative medicine at the University of Arizona Health Sciences Center. He was the founder and director of the University of Wisconsin Integrative Medicine Program and a tenured professor in the Department on Family Medicine at the UW School of Medicine and Public Health. He is now the professor and chair of the Department of Family & Community Medicine at the University of New Mexico School of Medicine in Albuquerque.

Dr. Rakel has received a number of teaching awards including the Baldwin E. Lloyd clinical teacher award, the UW Department of Family Medicine faculty excellence award, the Marc Hansen lecture award, the Resident Teacher-of-the-Year award, and the Leonard Tow award for compassionate care. He has also been accepted into the Gold Humanism Honor Society.

Author website available at davidrakel.com.

Susan Golant holds a master's degree in French literature and has been collaborating on nonfiction books—mostly on biopsychosocial issues—since 1983. She has more than forty books to her credit including three with former First Lady Rosalynn Carter. She has been honored with several awards for her books from the American Society of Journalists and Authors. Susan resides in Los Angeles with her husband, Dr. Mitch Golant.